W9-AMP-540

Beginner
Geography & Map Activities

Editors: Laurie Borman, Anne Ford
Writer: Carole Wicklander
Illustrator: Ewa Lonska

✿ RAND McNALLY

Beginner Geography and Map Activities

Copyright © 2005 by Rand McNally and Company

Published and printed in the United States of America

ISBN: 0-528-93469-4

For information on licensing and copyright permissions, please contact us at licensing@randmcnally.com.

10 9 8 7 6 5 4 3 2 1

A map is a drawing of Earth's surface. It shows the sizes and shapes of Earth's land and water.

Can you find land that is shaped like a boot? Circle it.

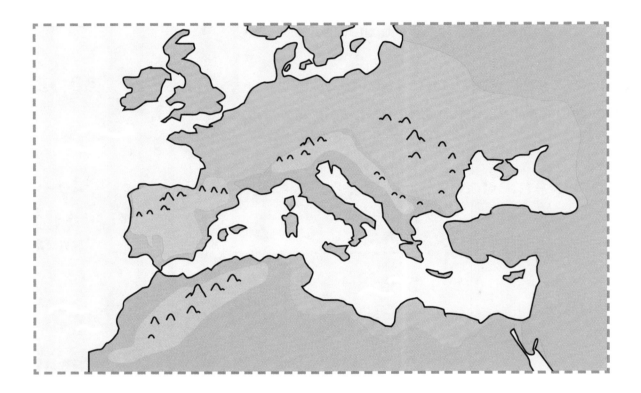

People use maps to . . .

- learn the names of Earth's land and water,
- locate places on Earth,
- find a route from one place to another,
- or maybe find a treasure!

Guess What

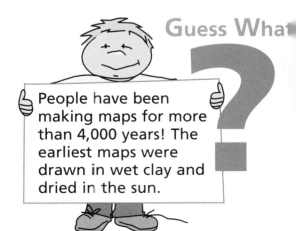

People have been making maps for more than 4,000 years! The earliest maps were drawn in wet clay and dried in the sun.

You are meeting your friend in the park. She has given you directions to the meeting place. Use her directions and this map to find the place where your friend is waiting.

Start at the entrance. Walk to the big tree. Walk 5 steps toward the slide to meet your friend.

Where are you meeting your friend? ✓

☐ at the picnic table

☐ at the water fountain

☐ at the ice cream stand

☐ at the bridge

There are many different kinds of maps. But most maps are alike in one way. They show places from a bird's-eye view.

Have you ever looked down from a window in a tall building? When you look at the earth from above, places and objects look smaller. When birds fly high in the air, that is how they see the earth.

Which picture shows a house from a bird's-eye view? ☑

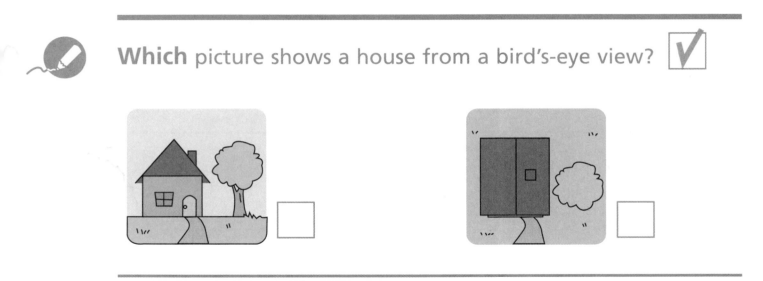

Maps can show many different things. To draw a map, a mapmaker needs to know how things look from a bird's-eye view.

These pictures show places from a bird's-eye view. Below is a list of the places they show. Write the name of each place under its picture. The first one has been done for you.

railroad tracks   **farm**   **town**
lake   **classroom**   **highway**

1. classroom   2. _____   3. _____

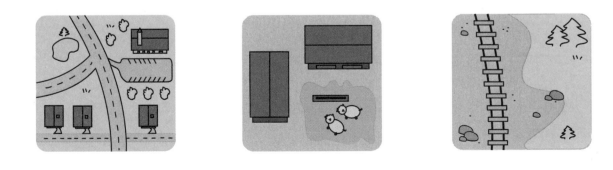

4. _____   5. _____   6. _____

If you see **+** in a math problem, you know you should add the numbers. **+** is a symbol that stands for addition.

Mapmakers use symbols for places and objects on maps. Sometimes a map symbol looks like the thing it stands for. For example, some maps show railroad tracks like this:

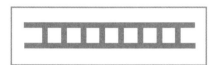

Other map symbols are lines or shapes. A map legend tells you what the symbols stand for.

Map Legend

 In this box, draw the symbol that stands for a park.

Maps can show many different areas: a neighborhood, a street, or even a room. Draw a map of a bedroom. First complete the map legend. Make up symbols for all the objects in the room and draw the symbols in the empty boxes below.

Map Legend

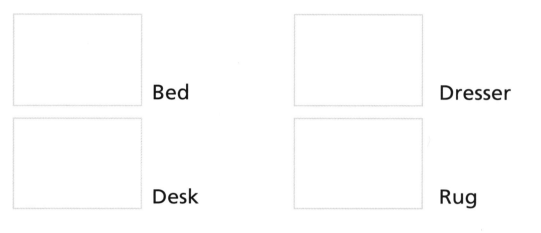

Bed

Dresser

Desk

Rug

Now draw a map in the box below to show where each object is located in the bedroom.

Bedroom Map

Early in the morning, you see the sun in the east. In the evening, the sun seems to go down in the west. East and west are directions. North and south are also directions.

A **compass rose** shows directions on a map. On many maps, north is at the top. What do the letters on the compass rose stand for? Write the answers on the lines below.

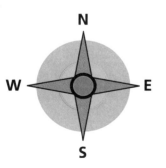

n _____   s _____   e _____   w _____

Here is a neighborhood map. Use the compass rose to answer the questions below.

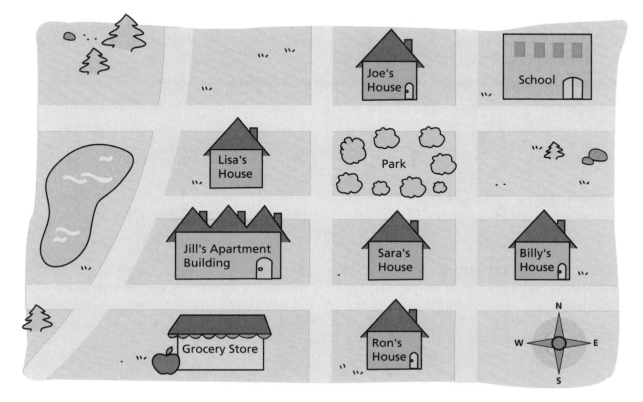

1. Whose house is east of Sara's house? _____.

2. Joe's house is _____ of the school.

3. Sara's house is _____ of the park.

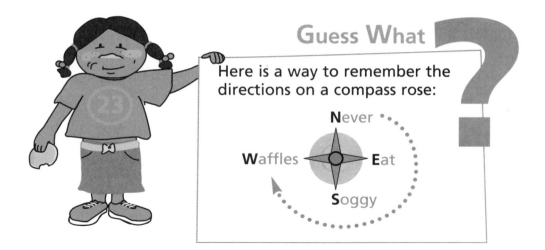

Guess What

Here is a way to remember the directions on a compass rose:

Never

Waffles   **E**at

Soggy

Some maps have a grid. A grid is made up of lines that cross each other to form boxes. If you know which box a location on a map is in, it is easier to find that location.

	1	2	3
A	d	p	f
B	l	i	n
C	a	e	c

1. Put one finger of your right hand on the number 2 at the top of the grid.

2. Put one finger of your left hand on the letter C at the left side of the grid.

3. Slide your right finger down and your left finger across until your fingers touch.

This is box **C-2**. What letter is in this box? _____

Find the letters that are in each of the following boxes. The first one has been done for you. What does a map grid help you do?

f									
A-3	B-2	B-3	A-1	C-1	A-2	B-1	C-1	C-3	C-2

Help! Someone has erased this map of a classroom. Copy the symbols from the legend onto the map. The letter and number for each symbol will tell you which box to draw each symbol in. The first one has been done for you.

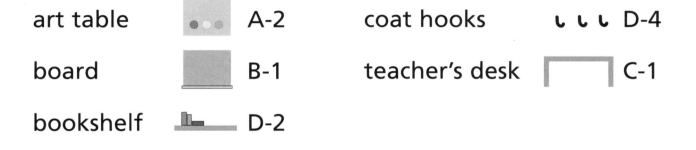

art table — A-2

board — B-1

bookshelf — D-2

coat hooks — D-4

teacher's desk — C-1

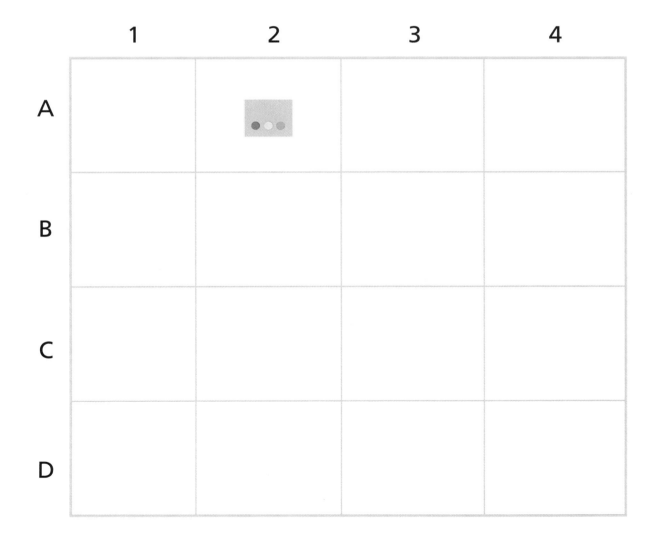

A map is much smaller than the size of the land and water it shows. Map scale helps you understand how distances on a map compare to real distances on Earth.

Here is an example of a bar scale on a map. It shows that 1 inch on a map stands for 100 miles on Earth.

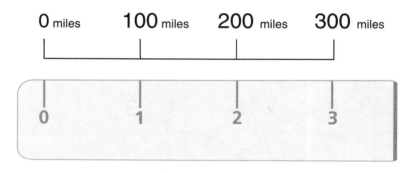

0 miles   100 miles   200 miles   300 miles

0   1   2   3

In the box below, use a ruler to draw a line that stands for 500 miles on Earth, using the scale above. How many inches long will your line be?

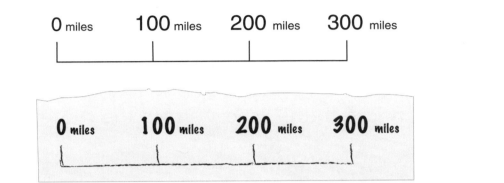

0 miles 100 miles 200 miles 300 miles

Copy this bar scale on a strip of paper. You will use it for the activity below.

If you wanted to find out how far apart Little Rock, Arkansas and Jackson, Mississippi are, you would:

- **Line up** the 0-mark on your paper bar scale with the star for Little Rock, Arkansas.

- **Line up** the other end of your paper bar scale so that it passes through Jackson, Mississippi. You can see that Jackson falls near the 200-mile mark on the paper bar scale.

- **About** how many miles apart are Little Rock and Jackson?

You can use a map to find a route from one place to another.

Find Frank's house on the map below. Here are directions from Frank's house to Hill School. Trace the route with your finger.

Go west on Water Street to First Avenue. Turn north and go two blocks to Hill Street.

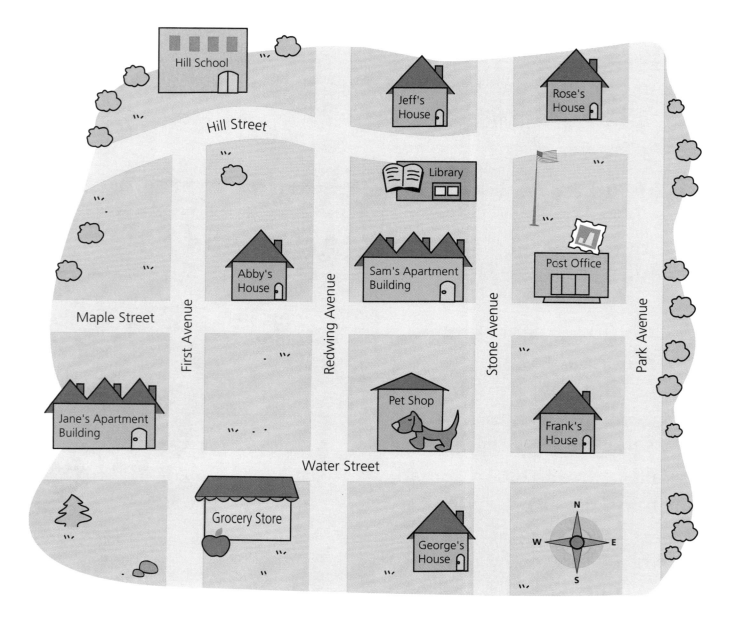

Use the map on page 16 to answer these questions.

1. Start at Jane's front door. Use a **red** crayon or colored pencil to trace the route from her apartment building to Hill School. What direction does she go on First Avenue?

   _____

2. Abby wants to go from her house to the post office. What streets will she cross?

   _____

   _____

3. Use a **blue** crayon or colored pencil to show two different routes George could take from his house to Hill School.

4. Sam is going shopping. He starts from his apartment building and goes west on Maple Street, south on Redwing Avenue, and east on Water Street. What store is he going to?

   _____

Guess What

In the 1970s, a man from Minnesota walked around the entire Earth. (Of course, he had to fly over the oceans.)

Both the map on this page and the map on the opposite page show the United States. But each map shows a different kind of information.

A physical map shows how high, low, flat, or hilly the land is. On it you can see mountains, valleys, and other landforms.

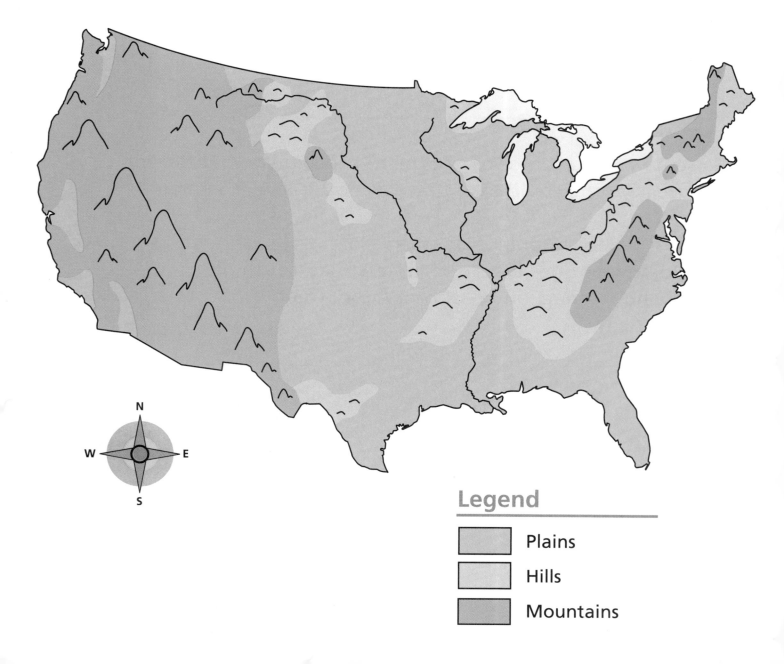

Legend

Plains

Hills

Mountains

A **political map** shows how people have divided the land into countries and states or provinces.

Look at the maps on pages 18 and 19. Which map would you use to . . .

1. . . . name the state that is south of Utah?

   _____

2. . . . find out which part of the United States has the most mountains? _____

Thematic maps show special kinds of information about a place, such as what the weather is like there or how many people live there.

Legend

⟨raising animals pattern⟩	Raising animals
⟨growing crops pattern⟩	Growing crops
⟨blank⟩	Making products to sell
⟨forestry pattern⟩	Forestry
⟨gray⟩	Little or no activity

This map shows how people in different parts of the United States earn a living. Use the map legend and the directions below to help you color the map with crayons or colored pencils. You can see that there is a place on the map that is already colored gray. That is a place where few people live.

Color green the places where people grow crops.
Color blue the places where people raise animals.
Color red the places where people make products to sell.
Color brown the places where people make a living from forests.

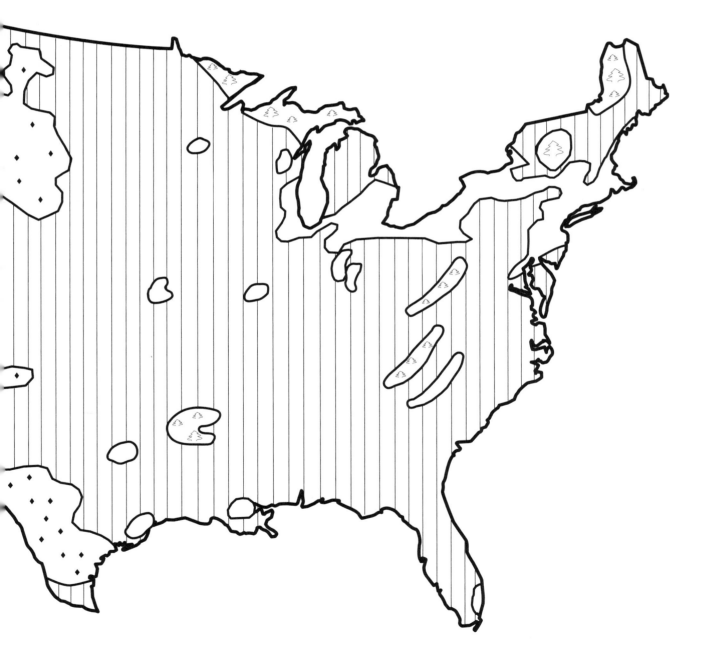

A map is a flat drawing of Earth's surface. A world map shows all of Earth's surface at once.

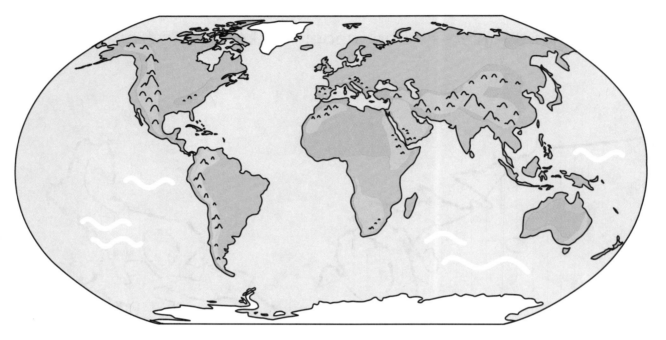

But Earth itself is not flat. It is shaped like a sphere, or ball. A globe is a model of Earth. It is also shaped like a sphere. When you turn a globe, you see different parts of Earth's land and water. If you look at Earth from outer space, it looks like a globe.

Maps and globes show the same things in different ways. Answer these riddles. Write **M** if the answer is map. Write **G** if the answer is globe. Write **B** if the answer is both.

What am I?

_____ **1.** When you look at me, you can see all of Earth's land and water at once.

_____ **2.** If you look at Earth from outer space, it looks like me.

_____ **3.** You can use me to learn about Earth's land and water.

_____ **4.** You have to turn me to see different parts of Earth.

_____ **5.** I am smaller than the land and water I show.

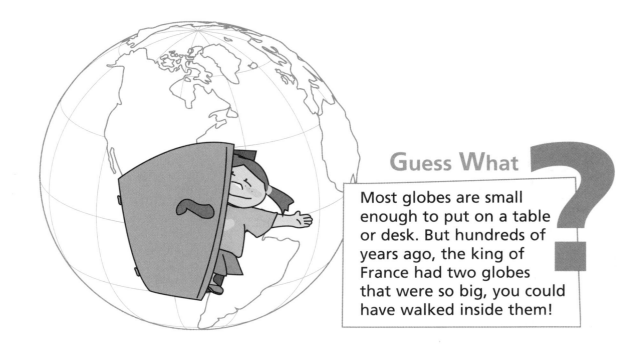

Guess What

Most globes are small enough to put on a table or desk. But hundreds of years ago, the king of France had two globes that were so big, you could have walked inside them!

The largest bodies of land on Earth are called continents. There are seven of them. Do you know which continent you live on?

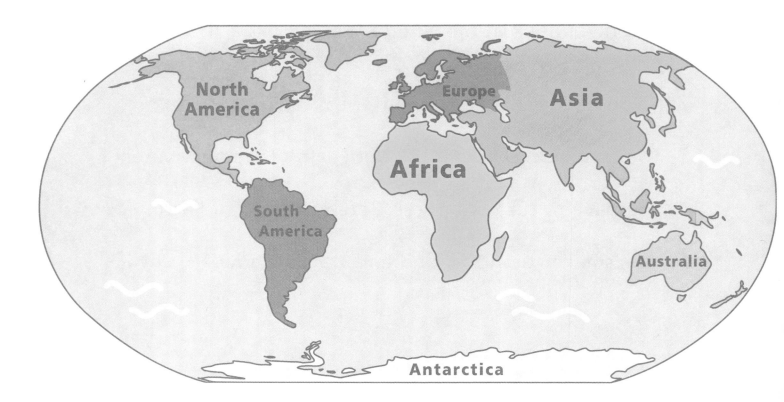

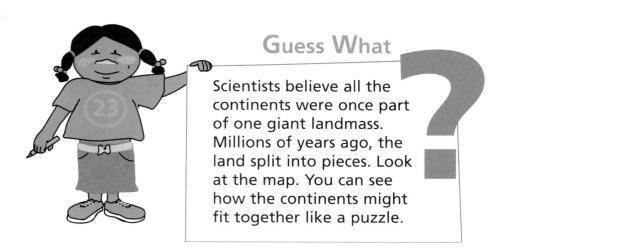

Guess What

Scientists believe all the continents were once part of one giant landmass. Millions of years ago, the land split into pieces. Look at the map. You can see how the continents might fit together like a puzzle.

Match the name of each continent with its shape. Use the world map on the opposite page to help you. Write the letter of the answer on the line. The first one has been done for you.

__e__ **1**. South America

a.

_____ **2**. Europe

b.

_____ **3**. Asia

c.

_____ **4**. Africa

d.

_____ **5**. Australia

e.

_____ **6**. North America

f.

Water covers almost all of Earth's surface. Earth's land divides the water into five main parts called oceans. Can you find the names of the oceans on this map?

 Circle the names of the oceans on this map.

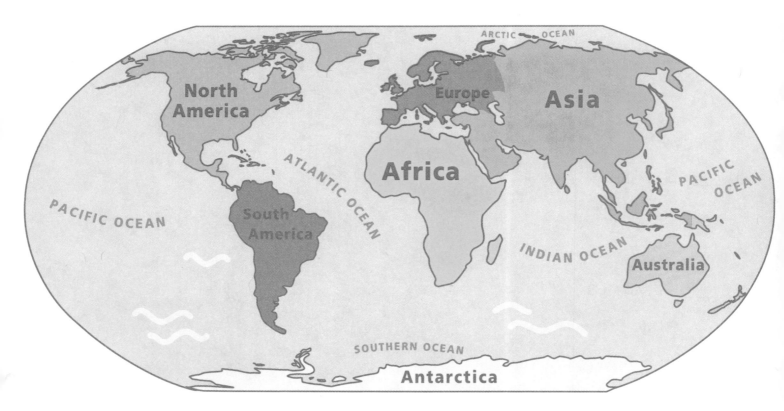

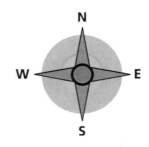

Use the map on the opposite page to help you name these oceans.

1. You can find my waters west of North America and South America and east of Asia and Australia.

   _____

2. If you travel from North America to Europe, you will have to cross my salty waters. _____

3. I am the smallest ocean. I am found north of Asia, Europe, and North America. _____

4. If you swim off the west coast of Australia, you are in my waters. _____

5. I am the ocean that surrounds Antarctica. _____

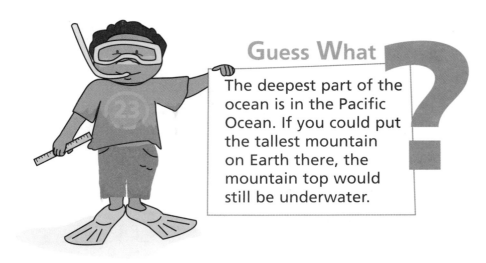

Guess What

The deepest part of the ocean is in the Pacific Ocean. If you could put the tallest mountain on Earth there, the mountain top would still be underwater.

Continents are divided into countries. This map shows the world's countries in different colors. What color is your country on this map? This map also shows country boundary lines. These lines show where a country begins or ends.

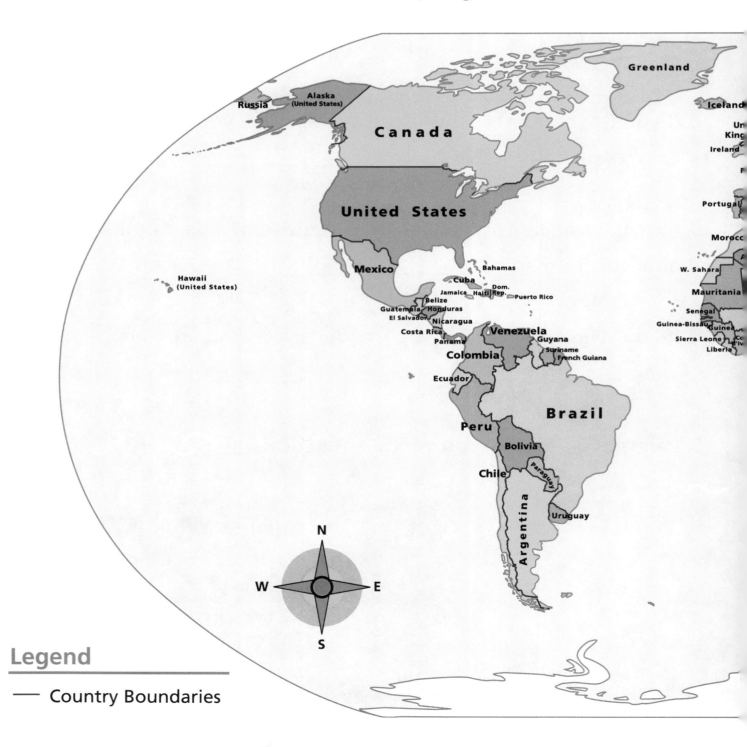

Legend

— Country Boundaries

Look at the country boundaries of the United States.

What country is north of the United States? _____

What country is south of the United States? _____

Each half of Earth is called a hemisphere.

If you divide Earth this way, the top half is the Northern Hemisphere. The bottom half is the Southern Hemisphere. Label the hemispheres in the boxes on this globe. Write **NH** on the Northern Hemisphere. Write **SH** on the Southern Hemisphere.

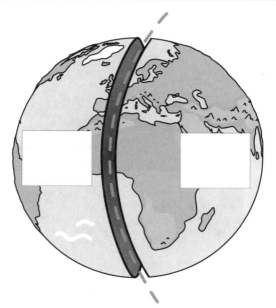

If you divide Earth this way, the right half is the Eastern Hemisphere. What do you think the left half is called? Label the hemispheres in the boxes on this globe.

Special lines on maps and globes divide the hemispheres.

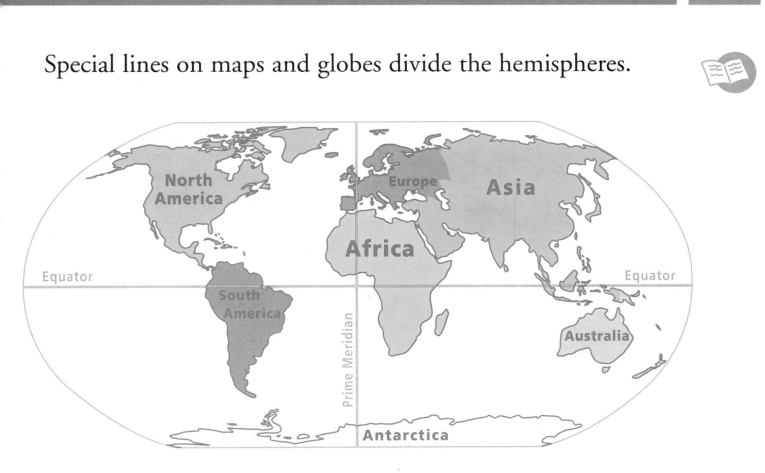

The **equator** is the line that divides the Northern Hemisphere from the Southern Hemisphere. Trace the equator on this map. Which three continents does it cross?

1. _____ 2. _____ 3. _____

The **prime meridian** is the line that (along with the 180° line of longitude) divides the Eastern Hemisphere from the Western Hemisphere. (You will learn about longitude lines on pages 34-37.) Trace the prime meridian on the map above. Which three continents does it cross?

1. _____ 2. _____ 3. _____

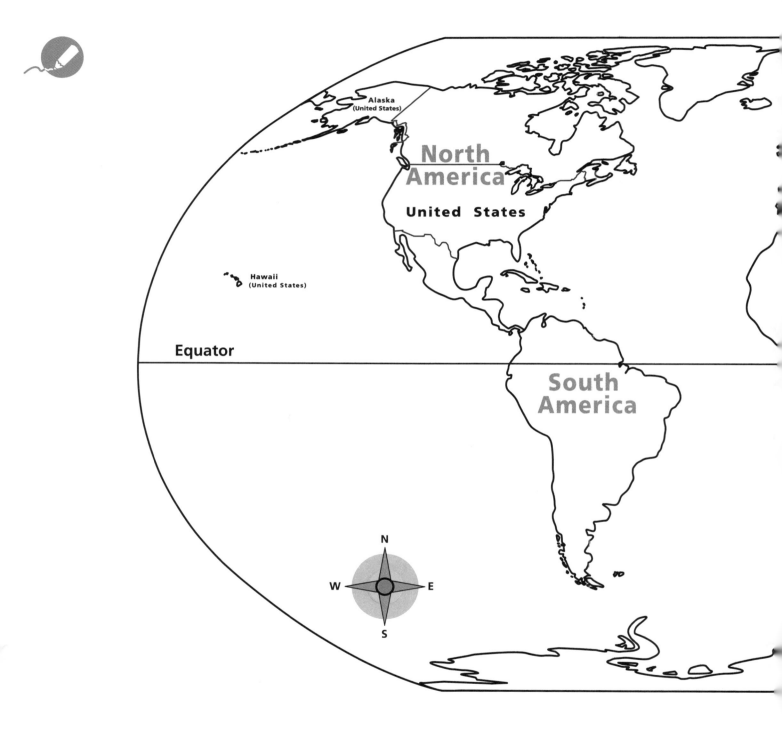

Follow the directions to show what you have learned about the world.

1. Find North America. Color it **green**.

2. Find the ocean east of North America. Label it **Atlantic Ocean**.

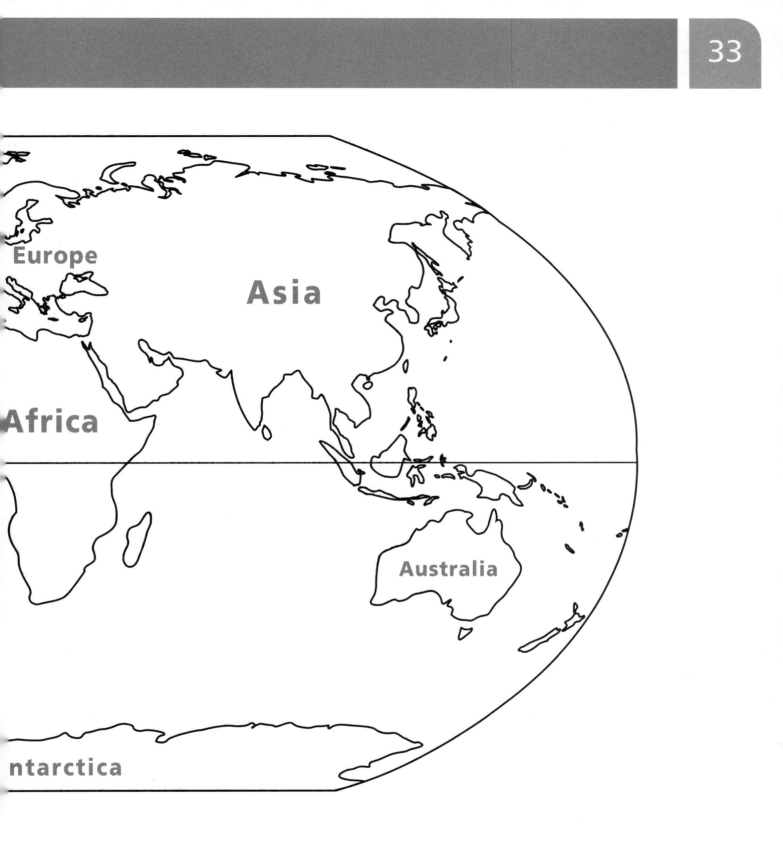

3. Find the ocean west of North America. Label it **Pacific Ocean**.

4. Find the United States. Trace its country boundaries in **black**.

5. Find the equator. Trace it in **brown**.

6. Color all the land in the Southern Hemisphere yellow.

Lines of latitude and longitude help you find places on a map or a globe. Lines of latitude run east and west. These lines are numbered along the sides of the map.

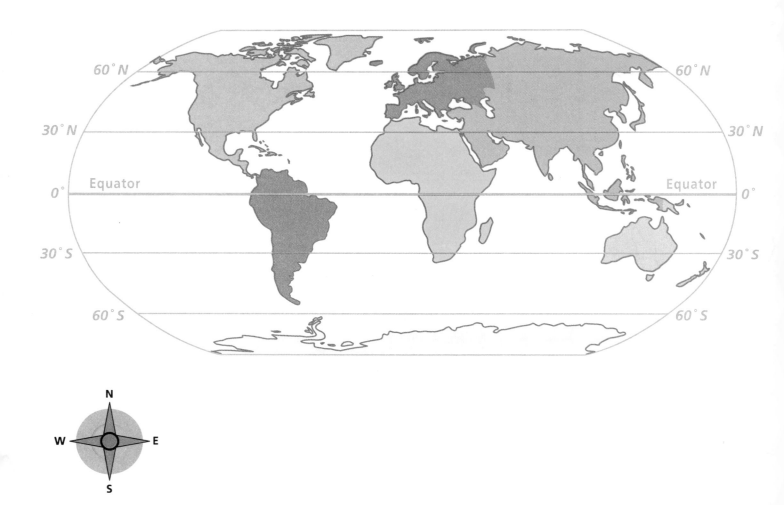

The equator is a line of latitude. Find the blue number next to the equator. The little circle next to the number is a degree sign. So we say the equator is zero degrees (0°) latitude.

Lines of longitude run north and south. These lines are labeled along the top and bottom of the map.

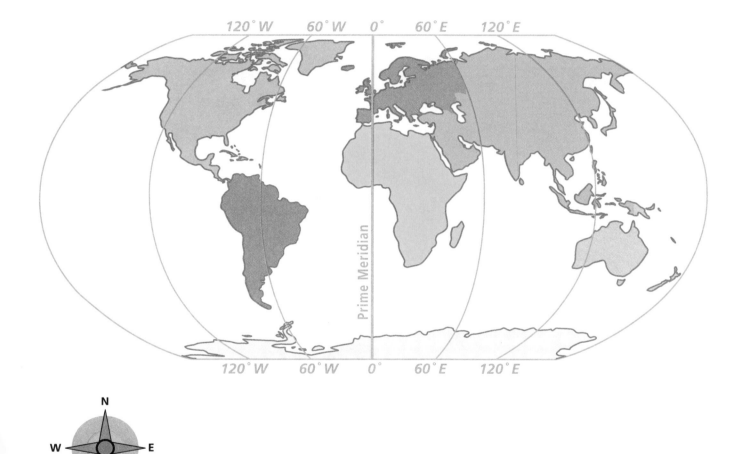

What is the name of the line at 0° longitude?

Lines of latitude and longitude form a grid on a map or a globe. A grid location is the point where a line of latitude and a line of longitude cross.

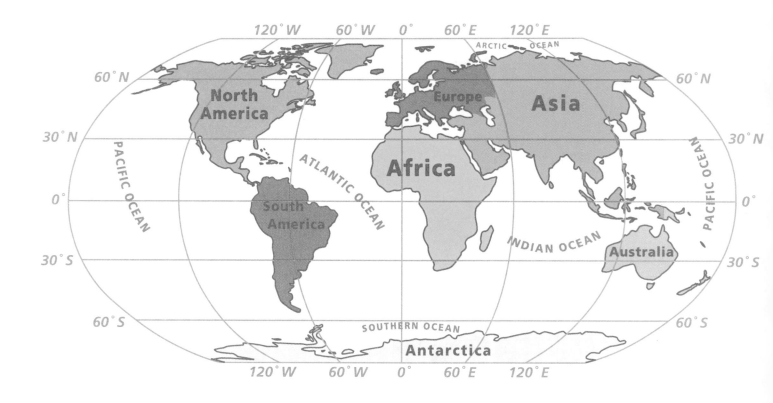

Put a finger of your left hand on 30°S on the left side of the map. Put a finger of your right hand on 60°W at the top of the map. Slide your right hand down and your left hand across until your fingers touch. The grid location is 30°S, 60°W. What continent are you touching?

Write the name of the continent or ocean that is found at each grid location on the lines next to it. Then use the letters in circles to complete the missing word in the sentence below. The first one has been started for you.

1. 60°S, 120°W

P A C I F I C __ __ Ⓞ __ __

2. 30°N, 60°E

__ __ __ Ⓞ

3. 30°S, 120°E

__ __ __ Ⓞ __ __ __ __

4. 30°S, 60°W

__ __ __ Ⓞ __ __   __ __ __ __ __ __

5. 60°N, 120°W

__ __ __ Ⓞ __   __ __ __ __ __ __

A latitude and longitude location is an

__ __ __ __ __ **address.**

What time is it right now where you live? Did you know that it is not the same time in different parts of the world?

The sun shines on different parts of the earth at different times. When it is nighttime on one side of the earth, it is daytime on the other.

There are six time zones in the United States. This map shows the time zones for all states except Alaska and Hawaii. Each zone has a time that is one hour different from the zones next to it.

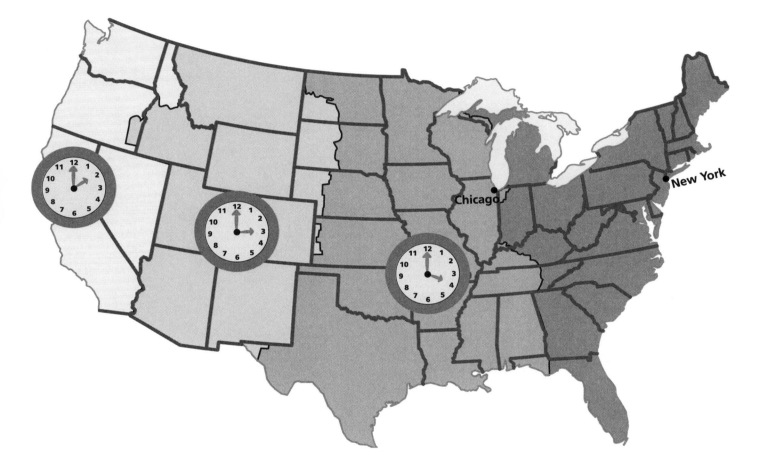

Notice that as the time zones go from left to right, the time gets later by one hour for every zone. If it is four o'clock in Chicago, what time do you think it is in New York?

Draw hands on the clock to show what time it is.

North America is the third largest continent on Earth. The United States, Canada, and Mexico are the largest countries in North America.

1. Use a **red** crayon to color the United States, including Alaska.

2. Use a **pink** crayon to color the country that borders the United States on the north.

3. Use a **purple** crayon to color the country that borders the United States on the south.

4. Central America is a part of North America. It is made up of Belize, Guatemala, Honduras, El Salvador, Nicaragua, Costa Rica, and Panama. Use a **yellow** crayon to color the countries of Central America.

5. An island is land that is surrounded by water. North America has many islands, including the world's largest island— Greenland. Use a **green** crayon to color Greenland.

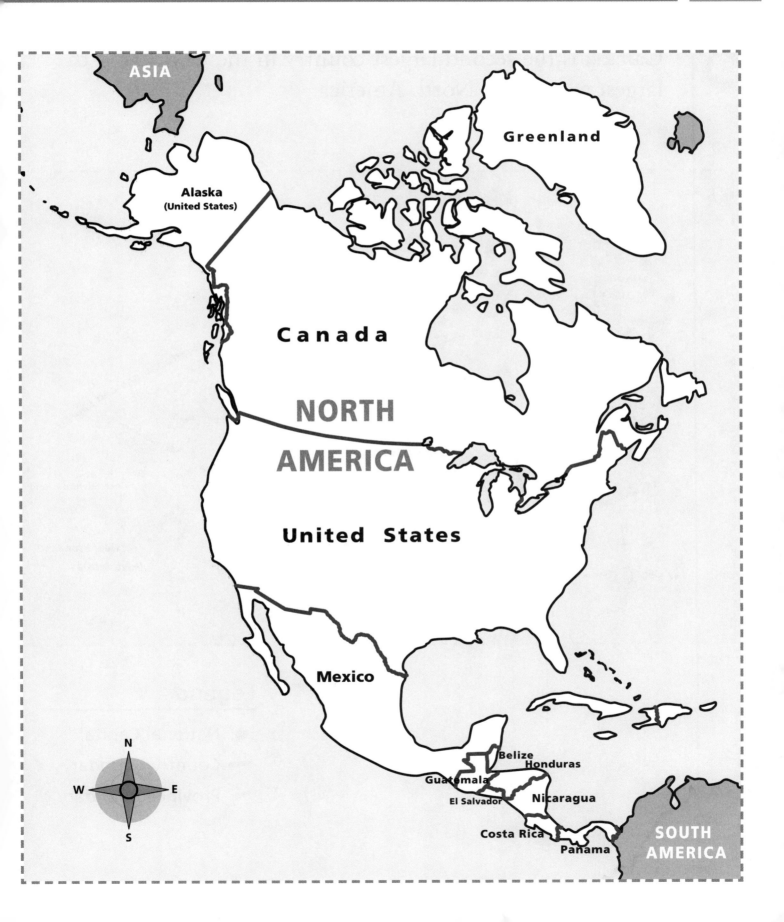

ASIA

Greenland

Alaska
(United States)

Canada

NORTH
AMERICA

United States

Mexico

Belize
Honduras
Guatemala
El Salvador
Nicaragua
Costa Rica
Panama

SOUTH
AMERICA

N
W E
S

Canada is the second largest country in the world. It is the largest country in North America.

Legend

⊛ National Capital

━ Country Boundary

━ Province Boundary

Canada is made up of ten provinces and three territories. Use the map on the opposite page to answer the questions below.

1. Which province borders the Pacific Ocean?

_____

2. What is the smallest province?

_____

3. What body of water borders Quebec on the west?

_____

4. Which province reaches furthest south?

_____

A national capital is the center of a country's government. Find the symbol for national capital in the map legend.

5. What city is Canada's national capital?

_____

Guess What

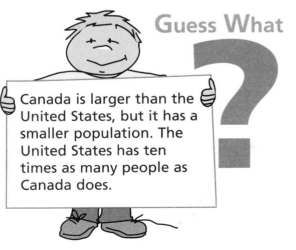

Canada is larger than the United States, but it has a smaller population. The United States has ten times as many people as Canada does.

Some Native Canadians called Inuit have lived in northern Canada for thousands of years. They once built igloos, traveled by dogsled, and made clothing from caribou skins. The Inuit today honor their history by teaching others about the old ways of life.

Owl Hop

Here is an Inuit game you can try with a friend. Place the top of one foot behind the knee of the other leg. Then hop on one foot as long as possible. You must hop on the same foot throughout the activity. Each hop must lift you off the floor. See who can hop longer, you or your friend.

Guess What

For a few months each winter, visitors to Quebec can stay in a real hotel made of ice. It has to be rebuilt every winter because it melts in the spring!

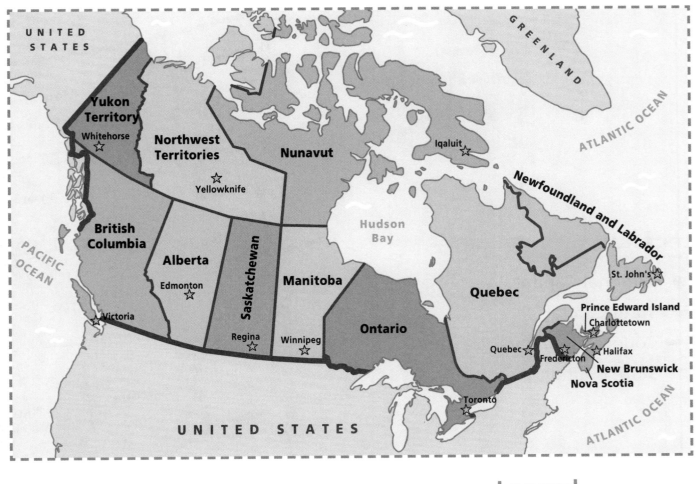

Legend

☆ Province Capital

Match each province or territory with its capital city.

___ **1.** Edmonton   **a.** Yukon Territory

___ **2.** Toronto   **b.** Nova Scotia

___ **3.** St. John's   **c.** Alberta

___ **4.** Whitehorse   **d.** Ontario

___ **5.** Iqaluit   **e.** Newfoundland and Labrador

___ **6.** Halifax   **f.** Nunavut

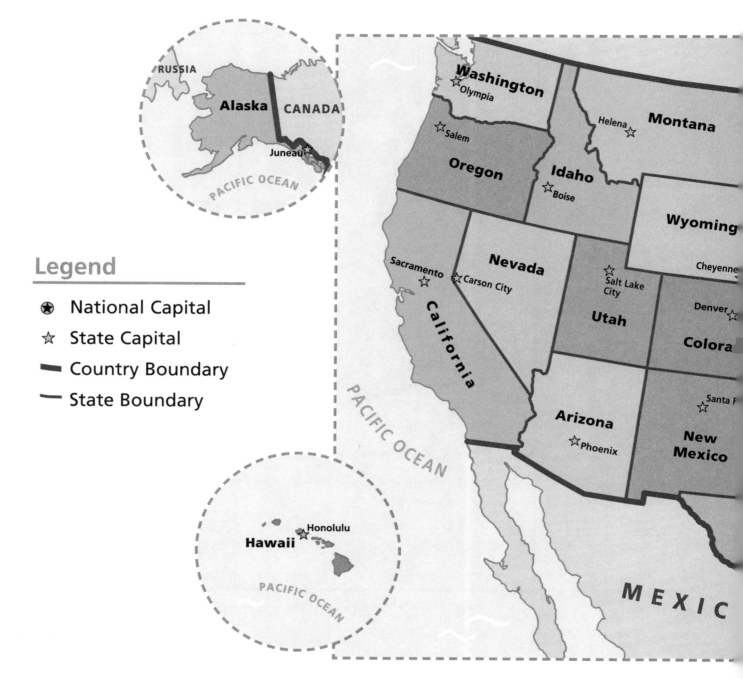

Legend

- ⊛ National Capital
- ☆ State Capital
- ▬ Country Boundary
- ▬ State Boundary

The United States is made up of fifty states. Most of the states border each other. But Alaska and Hawaii are separated from the rest of the states. You can see Alaska and Hawaii in the two small maps on this page.

1. What is the national capital of the United States?

_____

2. Each state has a capital that is the center of state government. Find the symbol for state capital in the map legend. What is the capital of Illinois? _____

State boundaries show you where each state begins and ends.

Use the map and the compass rose to help you solve these state riddles.

1. Nebraska is my neighbor to the north. Missouri is my neighbor to the east. Oklahoma is my neighbor to the south. Colorado is my neighbor to the west. What state am I?

   _____

2. Wisconsin is my neighbor to the east. Iowa is my neighbor to the south. What state am I?

   _____

3. Georgia and Alabama are my neighbors to the north. What state am I?

   _____

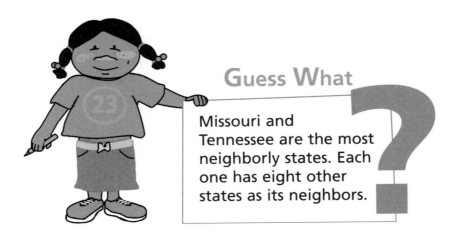

Guess What

Missouri and Tennessee are the most neighborly states. Each one has eight other states as its neighbors.

Boundary lines give each state its own special shape.

Find Oklahoma on the map. The western part of the state is called the panhandle.

Can you see why?

Use the map on the opposite page to help you identify these states. Write the name of each state under its outline.

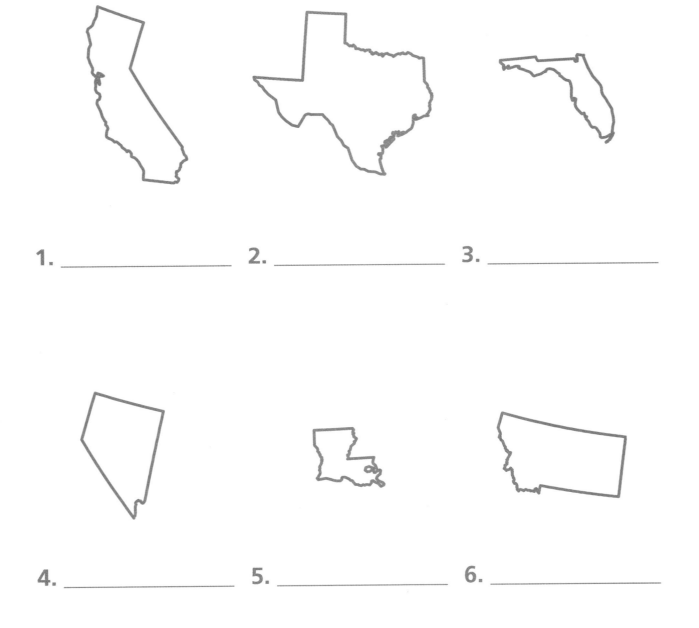

1. _____   2. _____   3. _____

4. _____   5. _____   6. _____

The United States has five very large lakes called the Great Lakes. Four of these lakes form part of the boundary between the United States and Canada.

Each Great Lake has its own name. The names are:
Lake Huron
Lake Ontario
Lake Michigan
Lake Erie
Lake Superior

Read the red letters above from top to bottom. What word will help you remember the names of the Great Lakes? Write it on the lines below.

_____   _____

The Mississippi River is the largest river in the United States. It forms the eastern boundaries of these states: Minnesota, Iowa, Missouri, Arkansas, Louisiana.
If you look at the boundaries of those states, you can see a man wearing a tall hat and boots.

Can you find the man on the map below? Color him in.

This climate map shows what the weather is like during the winter months in different parts of the United States. Look at the map legend to find out what the color of each area means.

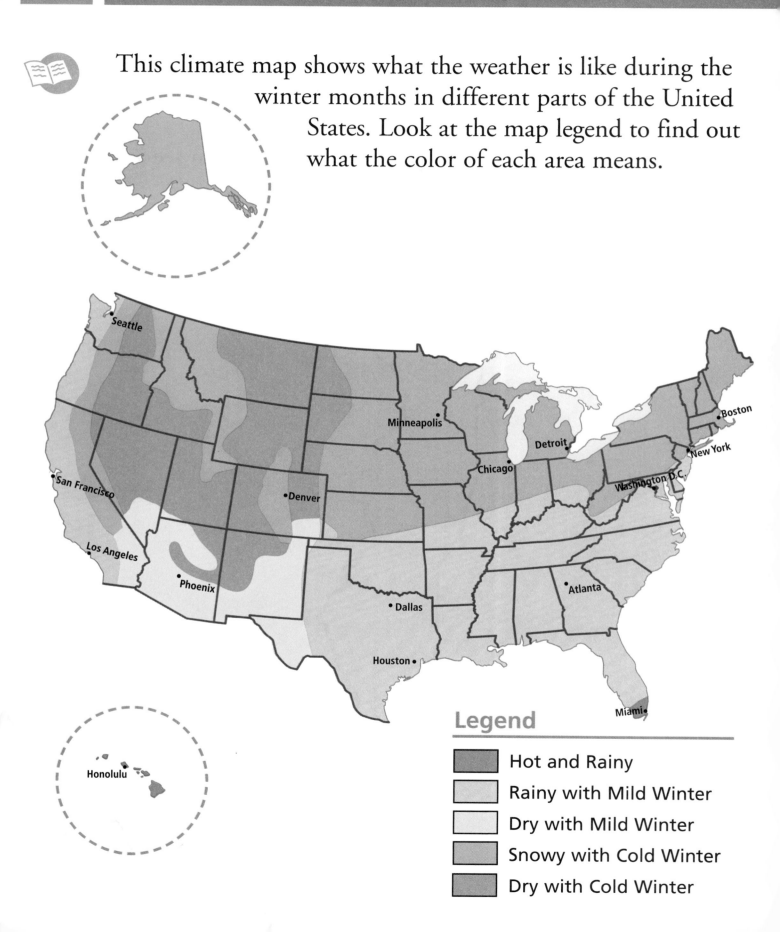

Legend

- Hot and Rainy
- Rainy with Mild Winter
- Dry with Mild Winter
- Snowy with Cold Winter
- Dry with Cold Winter

Draw a line from the name of each city below to the kind of clothes you would pack for a trip there during the winter months. Use the climate map to help you.

Boston

Phoenix

Miami

The United States can be divided into regions in different ways. This map shows one way.

The states are divided into regions according to their location in the United States.

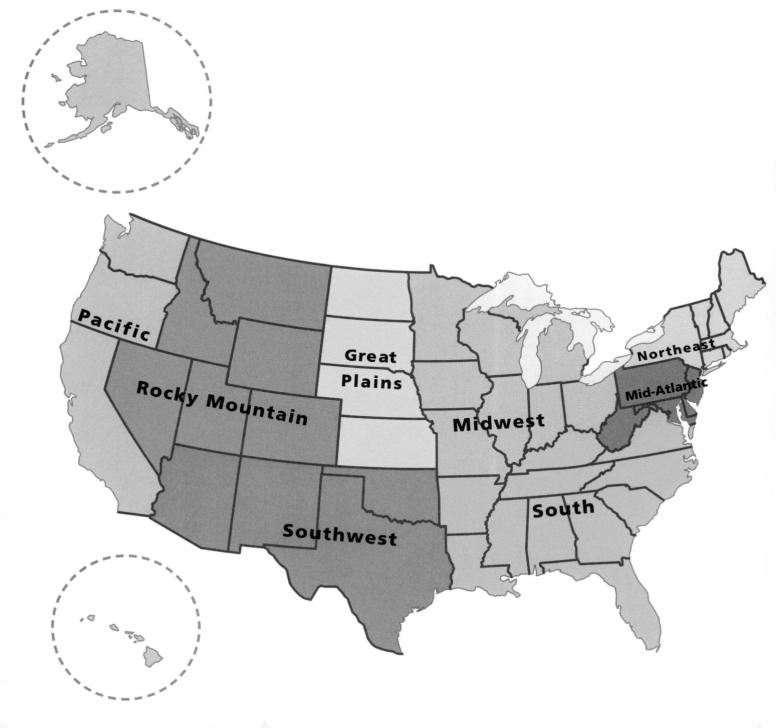

Can you unscramble the name of each region? Use the map to help you.

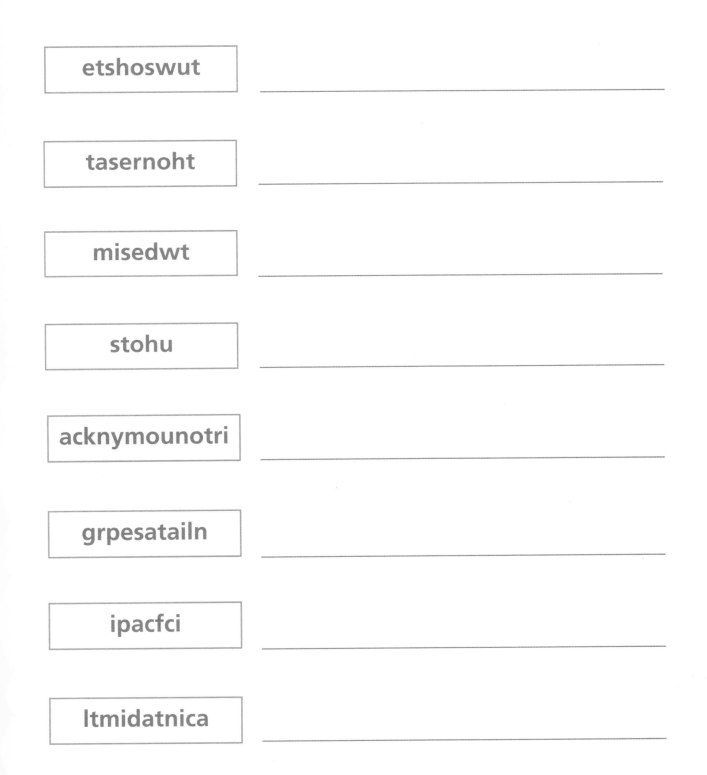

etshoswut

_____

tasernoht

_____

misedwt

_____

stohu

_____

acknymounotri

_____

grpesatailn

_____

ipacfci

_____

ltmidatnica

_____

The states in a region often share the same traditions, or customs that are handed down by the people who settled there. The people who live in a region today hold festivals to celebrate their traditions.

Can you match the name of the regional festival to its description?

Tulip Time Festival, Michigan

Cheyenne Frontier Days, Wyoming

St. Paul Winter Carnival, Minnesota

- This festival in the West includes nine rodeos.

- Visitors at this festival can see a palace carved out of ice.

- Thousands of tulips are in bloom during this celebration.

Guess What?

At the Great Cheese Festival in Wisconsin, there are cheese-eating contests and even carvings made out of cheese!

Mexico is the largest North American country south of the United States.

South of Mexico is Central America. The seven countries of Central America are located on a narrow piece of land between Mexico and South America.

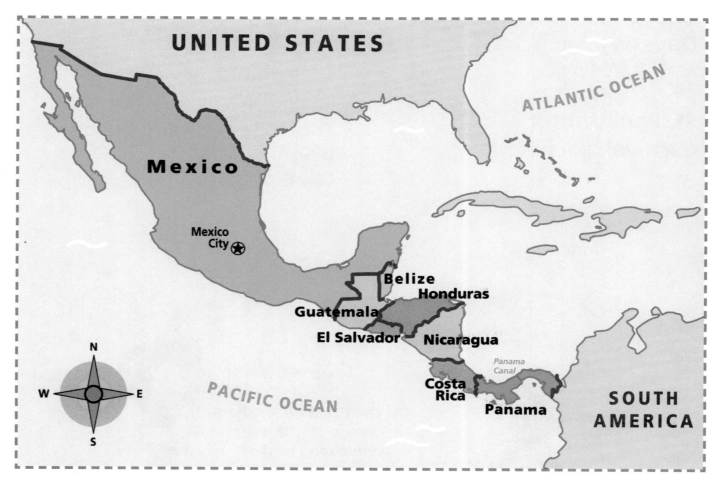

Legend

⊛ National Capital

Use the map on the opposite page to answer these questions.

1. Mexico's national capital is one of the largest cities in the world. What is its name?

_____

2. Which two Central American countries border Mexico?

_____

3. Which direction would you travel to get from Belize to El Salvador?

_____

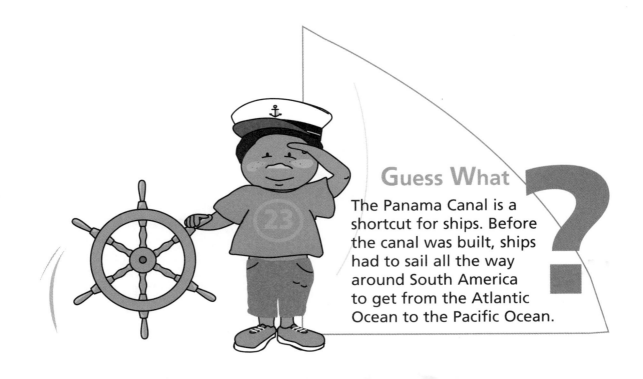

Guess What

The Panama Canal is a shortcut for ships. Before the canal was built, ships had to sail all the way around South America to get from the Atlantic Ocean to the Pacific Ocean.

Most people in Mexico and Central America speak Spanish. Learn the Spanish words for colors. Then color the map.

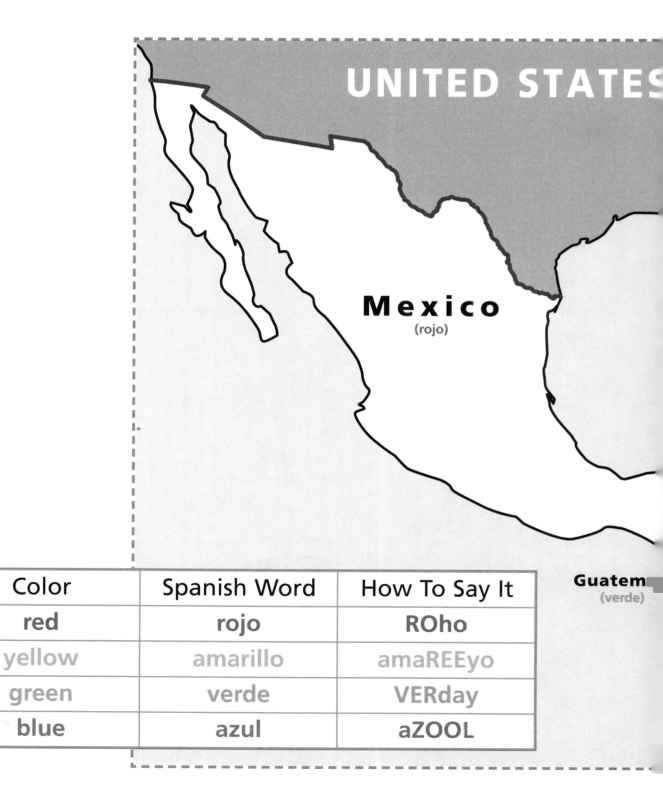

UNITED STATES

Mexico
(rojo)

Guatem
(verde)

Color	Spanish Word	How To Say It
red	rojo	ROho
yellow	amarillo	amaREEyo
green	verde	VERday
blue	azul	aZOOL

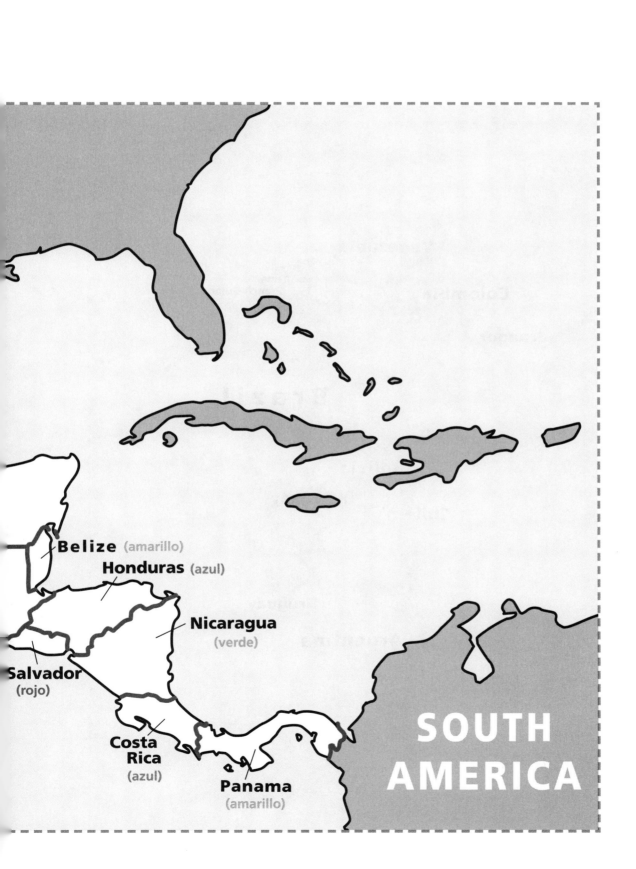

Belize (amarillo)

Honduras (azul)

Nicaragua
(verde)

Salvador
(rojo)

Costa Rica (azul)

Panama
(amarillo)

SOUTH AMERICA

South America has thirteen countries. Almost all of them have a seashore.

South America has thirteen countries. Use the map on the opposite page to answer these questions about the countries.

1. What is the largest country in South America?

_____

2. What two countries do NOT have a seashore?

_____

_____

3. What two countries border both Colombia and Peru?

_____

_____

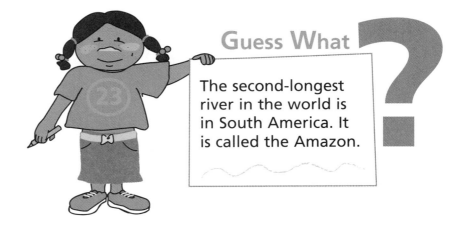

Guess What

The second-longest river in the world is in South America. It is called the Amazon.

The people of South America come from many different backgrounds. Some of them are Native Americans.

Make a Native American Rain Stick

A rain stick is a musical instrument from Chile in South America. Native Americans there once played the rain stick in hopes of bringing rain to the desert. You will need:

- a cardboard tube
- tape
- a cup of uncooked rice
- a few pieces of aluminum foil
- crayons or colored pencils

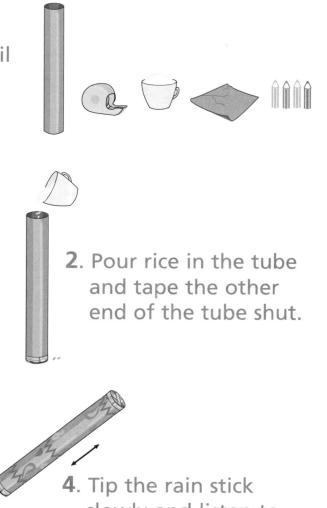

1. Tape one end of the tube shut. Crumple the foil into small balls and put them in the tube.

2. Pour rice in the tube and tape the other end of the tube shut.

3. Use paints or markers to decorate the tube.

4. Tip the rain stick slowly and listen to the sound of the rain.

Most people in South America speak Spanish. But in Brazil, the people speak Portuguese. Spanish and Portuguese have many words that look and sound similar. Can you draw a line from the Spanish word to the same word in Portuguese?

SPANISH   PORTUGUESE

escuela (school)
say esk-WAY-la

sapatas
say sah-PAH-toosh

zapatos (shoes)
say sah-PAH-toes

livro
say LEE-vroo

libro (book)
say LEE-bro

escola
say ish-KOH-lah

Most people in South America live in cities near the coast. South America has some of the largest cities in the world.

Caracas

Venezuela

Georgetown

Paramaribo

Bogota

Guyana Cayenne

Suriname

French Guiana

Colombia

Quito

Ecuador

Peru

Andes Mountains

Brazil

Lima

Bolivia

La Paz

Brasilia

Sucre

Paraguay

Asuncion

Rio de Janeiro
Sao Paulo

Argentina

Uruguay

Santiago

Buenos Aires

Montevideo

Chile

Legend

⊛ National Capital

● City

Look at the map on the opposite page. Then try to answer the questions below. Try not to peek!

1. This is the capital of Argentina. Its name means "fair winds."

_____

2. This city in Colombia is in the mountains.

_____

3. This is the capital of the largest country in South America.

_____

4. This city is the capital of Peru.

_____

5. This city lies north of all the other cities on the map.

_____

In South America, soccer is the most popular sport. But it is not called soccer there. It is called futbol (say FOOT-bol).

Many South Americans enjoy meat pies called empanadas (say em-pah-NAH-dahs).

People in Brazil celebrate New Year's Eve by putting candles and flowers on the beaches.

Guess What

Some people in Brazil like to put bananas and cinnamon on pizza!

South America has many interesting animals.

Llamas live in the mountains. Watch out, they spit!

Jaguars are large spotted cats that live in forests or grasslands where they can hide.

Toucans are colorful birds that live in rain forests. (You can read more about rain forests on page 72.)

Now that you have learned about three South American animals, find and circle their names in this puzzle.

```
H I E Z L K
E R J F L G
N L A D A S
T O G J M H
T O U C A N
B M A Q B V
J E R D J C
```

A rain forest is a forest that receives at least 100 inches of rain each year. (That's about twice as much rain as New York City gets each year!) The rain forest in South America is the largest in the world. It has thousands of fascinating and beautiful plants, animals, and insects.

But the rain forest is slowly disappearing, and so are many of its plants and animals. The rain forest is being cleared through something called deforestation. Deforestation means that people are cutting down trees so they can use the land for other things, like farming.

Color the map on the next page to show how much of the rain forest has disappeared. Color the areas of deforestation **red**. Color the areas of rain forest **green**. Use the legend to help you.

Legend

🌳	Rain forest
▧	Deforestation

Europe is a small continent, but it has many countries. It has more people than any continent except Asia. Some of the world's most famous cities are in Europe.

Use the map on the opposite page to help you identify some of Europe's countries.

1. What country borders Sweden on the east?

_____

2. If you are traveling from France to Portugal, what country will you pass through?

_____

3. Which country is shaped like a boot?

_____

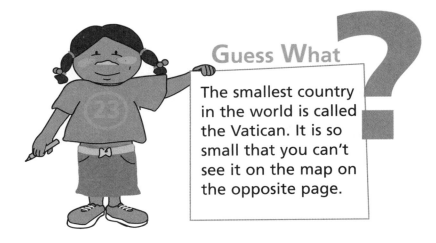

Guess What?

The smallest country in the world is called the Vatican. It is so small that you can't see it on the map on the opposite page.

A landmark is a famous building that many people recognize. Europe has many landmarks that are known all over the world.

Visitors can go to the top of the Eiffel Tower in France.

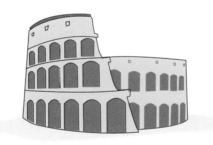

The Colosseum is a large outdoor theater that was built in Italy 2,000 years ago.

Neuschwanstein Castle looks like it belongs in a fairy tale. It was built in Germany more than 100 years ago.

Make a map legend for this map. In the boxes underneath the map, create a symbol for each landmark shown on the opposite page. Then draw the symbol in the correct place on the map.

Legend

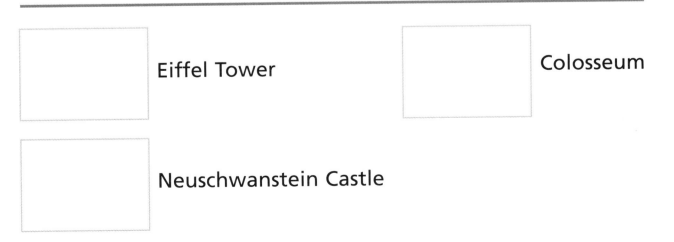

Eiffel Tower

Colosseum

Neuschwanstein Castle

This map shows how many people live in Europe. You can look at it and see which parts of Europe are the most crowded.

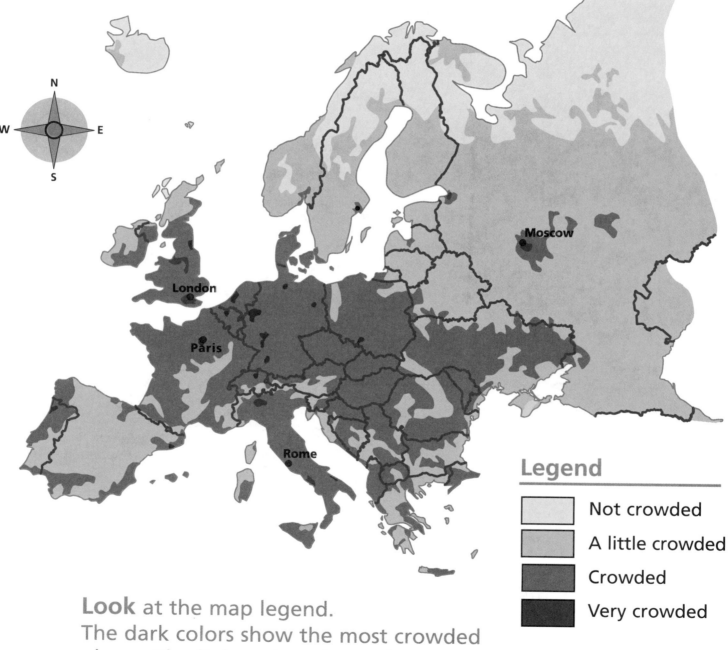

Legend

▢	Not crowded
▨	A little crowded
▨	Crowded
▉	Very crowded

Look at the map legend.
The dark colors show the most crowded places. The light colors show places that are less crowded.

Is northern Europe more crowded or less crowded than the rest of the continent? _____

The map on the opposite page shows the location of some of Europe's major cities. The list below shows the population of these cities.

Moscow   **10** million people
London   **7** million people
Rome   **2** million people
Paris   **10** million people

The bar graph below shows that 10 million people live in Moscow. Finish the bar graph. Color each city's bar to show how many millions of people live there. The first one has been done for you.

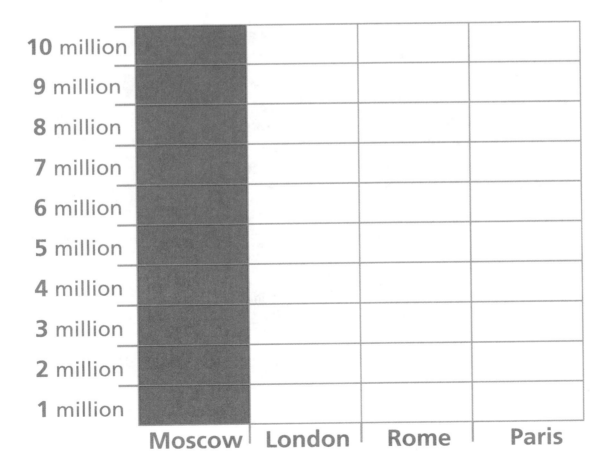

Europe's rivers are major transportation routes. They also supply water for homes and farms.

Europe's mountains provide beautiful scenery. Some of them form boundaries between countries.

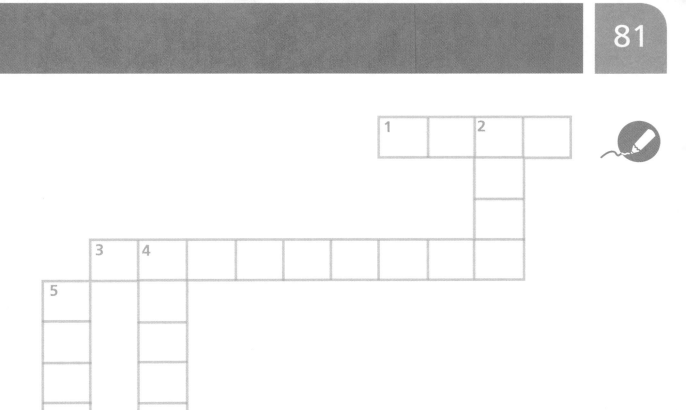

Use the map on the opposite page to help you complete this crossword puzzle.

Across

1. These mountains are in Russia.
3. These mountains cover most of Italy.
6. This is the most famous river in England. It empties into the North Sea.

Down

2. These mountains cover most of Switzerland.
4. These mountains form the boundary between France and Spain.
5. This is Europe's longest river. It flows through Russia to the Caspian Sea.

Many countries in Europe have palaces. Palaces are large, beautiful buildings where kings and queens live. The Queen of England lives in Buckingham Palace in London.

Some countries no longer have kings and queens, but you can still see the palaces where they used to live.

Sometimes palaces have gardens that are laid out like a maze. Visitors enjoy trying to find their way through the maze.

Guess What

?

The largest palace in Europe is the Royal Palace in Madrid, Spain. It has 44 staircases!

Can you find your way through this maze to the palace?

Enter
Here ▶

Africa is the second largest continent, and it has more countries than any other continent.

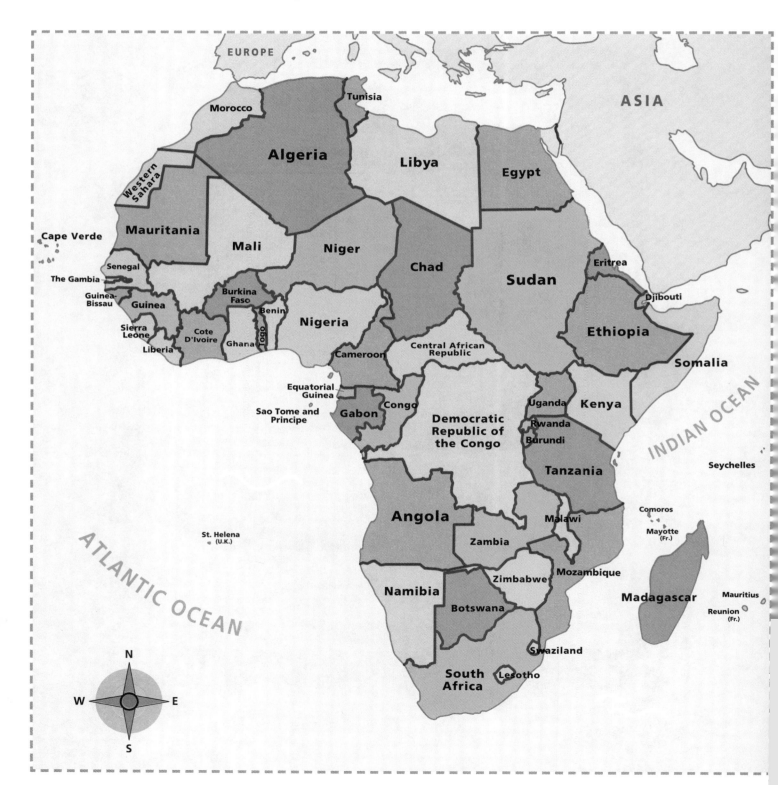

Pretend you are traveling in Africa and answer the questions below. Use the map on the previous page to help you.

1. If you are in Botswana and you want to go to Zambia, which direction will you travel?

_____

2. If you are in Mozambique and want to travel to Madagascar, will you buy a train ticket or a boat ticket?

_____

3. If you are in Morocco, what other continent are you close to?

_____

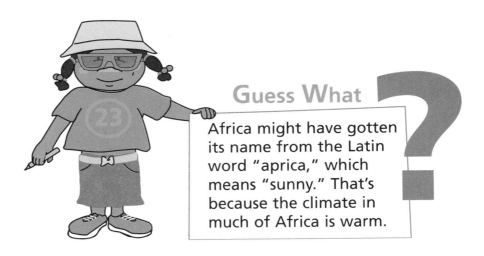

Guess What

Africa might have gotten its name from the Latin word "aprica," which means "sunny." That's because the climate in much of Africa is warm.

Africa has many kinds of environments. Some are hot, dry, and sandy. Others are rainy, with lots of trees and plants.

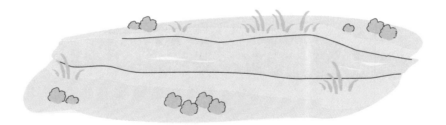

Animals that live in Africa adapt to their environment. Read the descriptions of animals on the next page. Then draw a line from each animal to the environment it lives in.

Camels can go without water for three or four days. They have long eyelashes that protect their eyes from blowing sand.

Colobus monkeys have long black-and-white fur. They eat leaves and insects, and they like to swing from tree to tree.

Hippos have large feet that help them walk along river bottoms. They eat grasses that grow near water.

Egypt became an important kingdom in Africa about 5,000 years ago. Egyptian farmers raised crops along the Nile River. Egyptian builders made huge stone pyramids that are still standing.

Egyptians used a form of writing called **hieroglyphics** (say HI-ro-GLIH-fix).

You can write your name in hieroglyphics. Look at the chart on the opposite page to find the symbols for each letter of your name. Then write the symbols in the box under the chart.

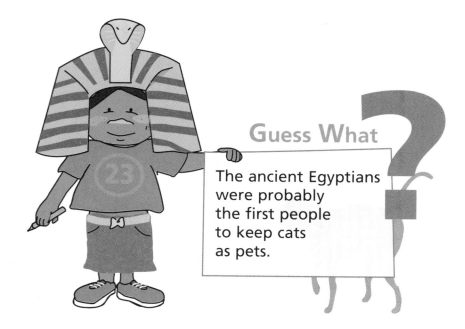

Guess What?

The ancient Egyptians were probably the first people to keep cats as pets.

About 150 years ago, ships carrying people and goods from Europe had to travel around Africa to get to India. Find the United Kingdom and India on the map.

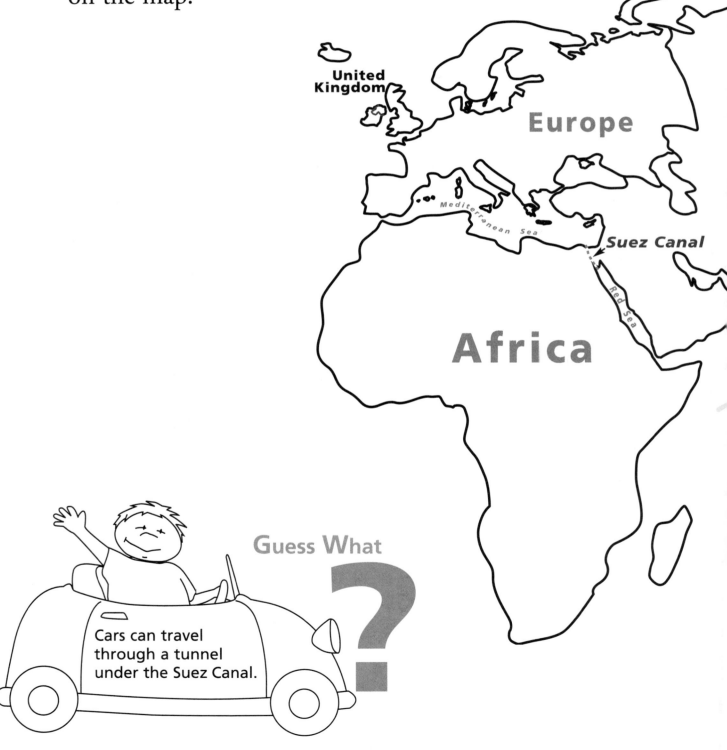

United Kingdom

Europe

Mediterranean Sea

Suez Canal

Red Sea

Africa

Guess What

?

Cars can travel through a tunnel under the Suez Canal.

In 1869, the Suez Canal was built to connect the Mediterranean Sea and the Red Sea. Find the Suez Canal on the map.

Asia

India

Use a **blue** crayon or marker to show the route a ship could use to sail from the United Kingdom to India through the Suez Canal.

Then use a **red** crayon or marker to show the route a ship would have to use from the United Kingdom to India if the canal did not exist. Which route is shorter?

It's time to practice using map grids. Do you remember how to use them? Look at page 12 if you need help.

Use the map grid on the opposite page to match each country with its location.

_____ **1**. B-1   **a**. Tunisia

_____ **2**. A-3   **b**. Burundi

_____ **3**. C-4   **c**. Djibouti

_____ **4**. D-4   **d**. Senegal

_____ **5**. B-5   **e**. Malawi

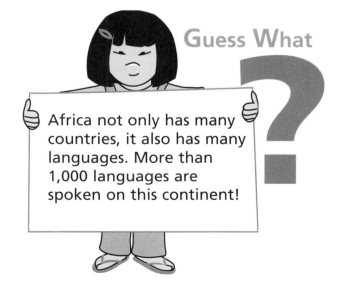

Guess What

?

Africa not only has many countries, it also has many languages. More than 1,000 languages are spoken on this continent!

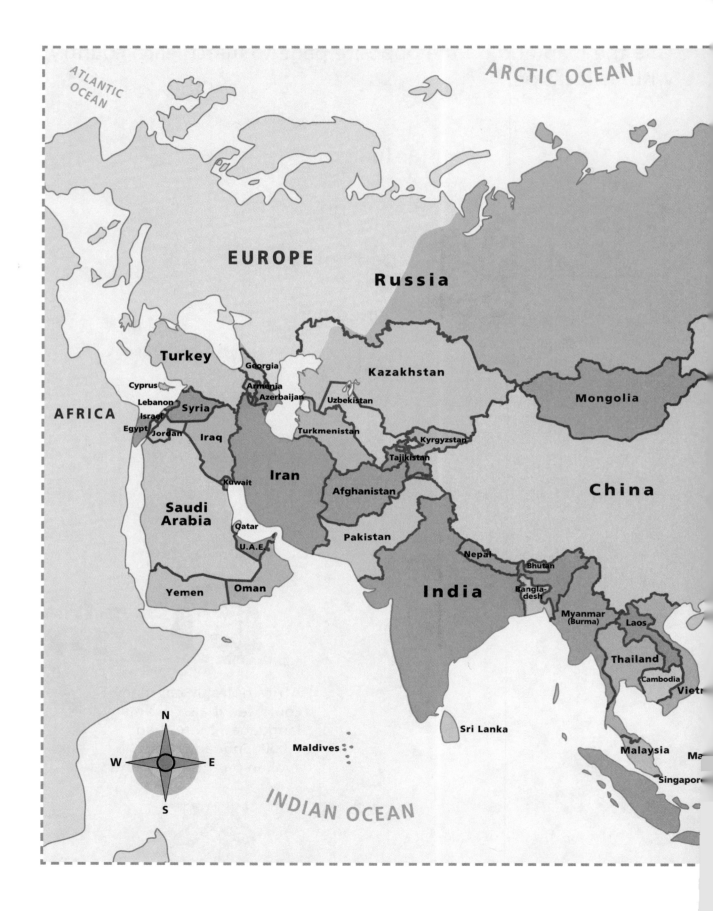

ATLANTIC OCEAN

ARCTIC OCEAN

EUROPE

Russia

Turkey

Georgia

Cyprus

Armenia

Azerbaijan

Kazakhstan

Mongolia

Lebanon

Syria

Uzbekistan

AFRICA

Israel

Egypt

Jordan

Iraq

Turkmenistan

Kyrgyzstan

Tajikistan

China

Kuwait

Iran

Afghanistan

Saudi Arabia

Qatar

Pakistan

U.A.E.

Nepal

Bhutan

Yemen

Oman

India

Bangla-desh

Myanmar (Burma)

Laos

Thailand

Cambodia

Vietn

N

W   E

S

Sri Lanka

Maldives

Malaysia

Ma

Singapore

INDIAN OCEAN

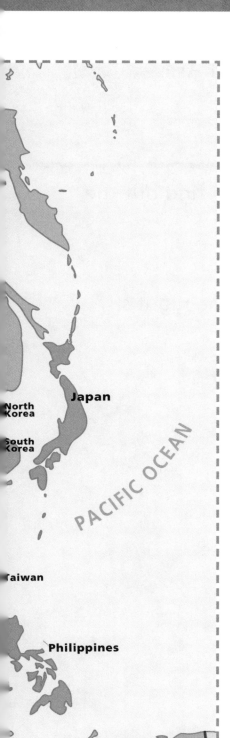

Asia is the largest continent in land size. It also has more people than any other continent. More than half the world's people live in Asia.

---

1. What three oceans border Asia?

_____

_____

_____

2. Indonesia is an island country. It is farther south than any other Asian country. What Asian country is farthest north?

_____

Many things we use today were invented in Asia long ago.

Read the clues and unscramble the words to find out the names of some inventions from Asia.

1. These brightly colored lights explode in the night sky for holidays and other special events.

   r r w f e i k o s

   ___ ___ ___ ___ ___ ___ ___ ___ ___

2. On a windy day, you might fly one of these.

   iket

   ___ ___ ___ ___

3. If you make a list or do your homework, you are using this invention from Asia.

   rppae

   ___ ___ ___ ___ ___

Tangram is a game invented in China.

Trace the diagram below onto a piece of paper. Then cut the paper along the lines so you have 7 pieces. You can arrange the pieces to make different shapes.

Can you make these animal shapes?

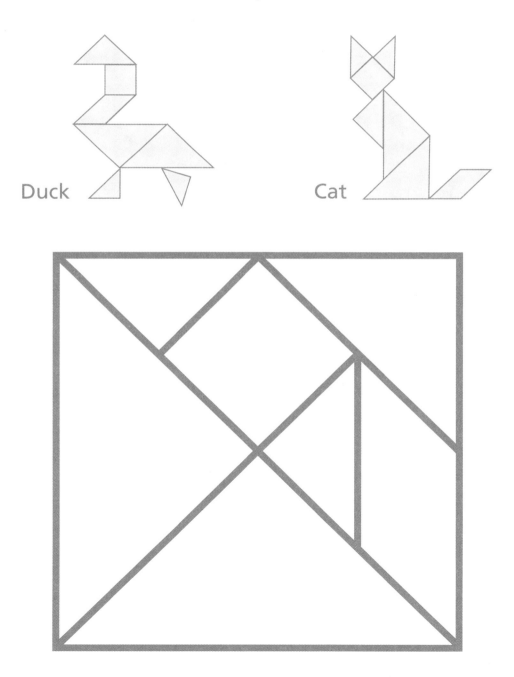

Duck

Cat

Asia has many different physical features, or places made by nature. Mountains and lakes are two examples of physical features. Asia's Mount Everest is the world's highest mountain.

Legend

	Plains
	Hills
	Mountains
▲	Mount Everest

Find the symbol for Mount Everest in the map legend. Then find it on the map.

Climb Mount Everest by answering these questions about other physical features of Asia. Start with the question at the bottom and work your way to the top.

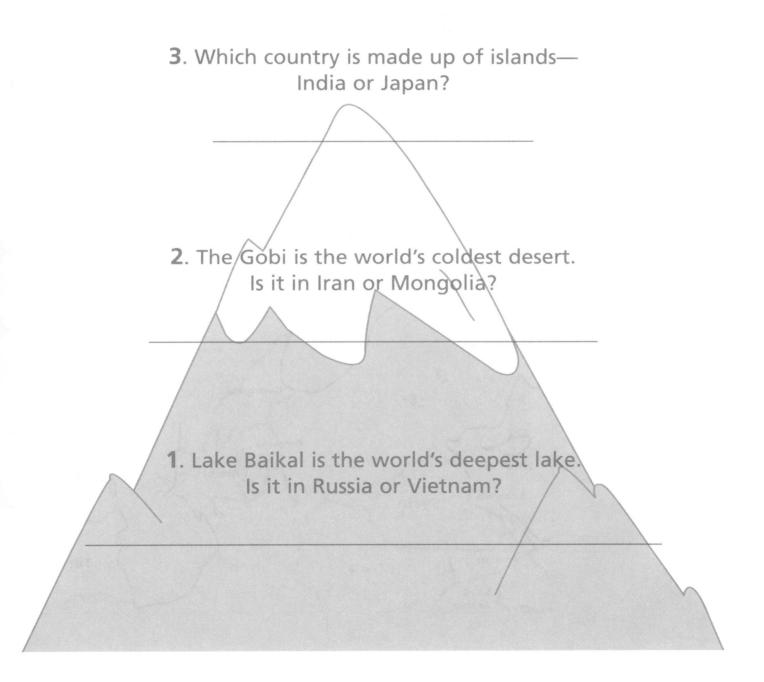

3. Which country is made up of islands—India or Japan?

_____

2. The Gobi is the world's coldest desert. Is it in Iran or Mongolia?

_____

1. Lake Baikal is the world's deepest lake. Is it in Russia or Vietnam?

_____

Asia shares the same landmass with Europe. The Ural Mountains are part of the dividing line between Asia and Europe. Some countries have land on both continents.

The land on one side of the grey line is Europe. The land on the other side is Asia.

Color Europe **yellow**. **Color** Asia **red**.

How many countries are part red and part yellow? _____

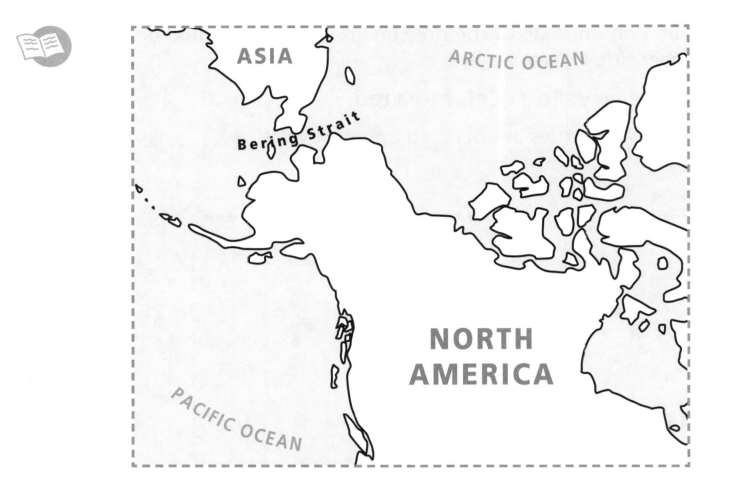

The Bering Strait is a waterway that separates Asia and North America. The two continents are not very far apart.

Scientists believe that thousands of years ago, there was a land bridge where the Bering Strait is now. People from Asia may have crossed the land bridge to come to North America.

On the map, draw arrows to show the shortest route from Asia to North America across the Bering Strait.

Asia has many beautiful animals. But some of those animals are endangered. That means they are disappearing because they do not have enough food or land.

Connect the dots below to make a picture of one of Asia's endangered animals. Then color it in.

What is the name of this animal? _____

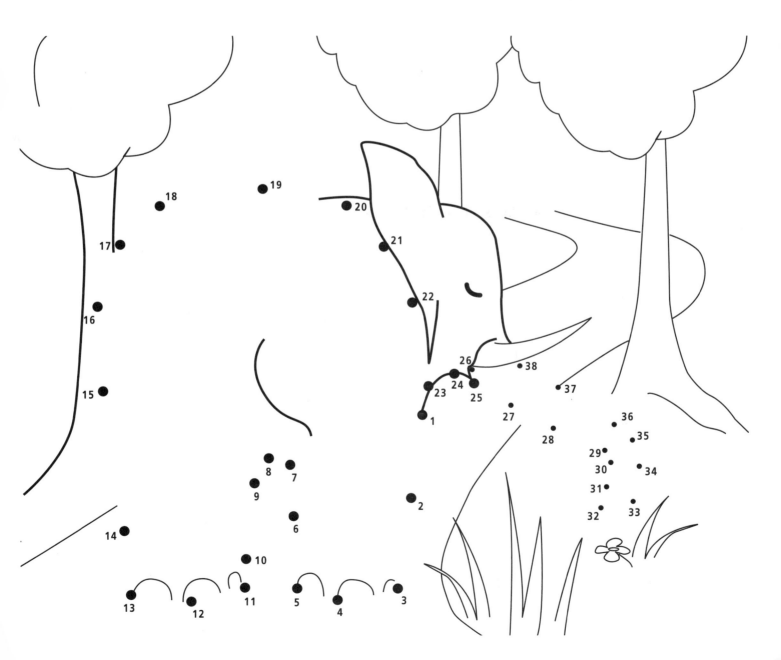

Australia is the smallest continent. It is the only continent that is also a country.

The island of Tasmania is part of Australia. New Zealand is east and south of Australia. It is a separate country.

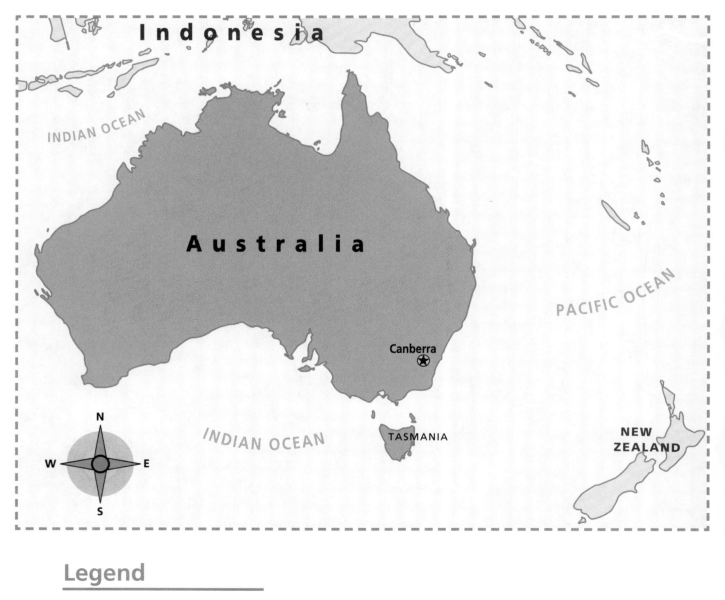

Legend

⊛ National Capital

Use the map on the opposite page to help you answer questions about Australia.

1. If you are on the island of Tasmania and want to go to New Zealand, which direction will you travel?

_____

2. What is the capital of Australia?

_____

3. If you sail from Indonesia to northern Australia, which ocean will you cross?

_____

Guess What

All of Australia lies south of the equator. That's why its nickname is the Land Down Under.

The Australian outback is the large dry region in the middle of the continent. There are few towns in the outback.

People there live on cattle or sheep ranches called stations. They sometimes use small airplanes to travel from place to place.

Children who live on stations don't have schools nearby. So instead they study at home and use computers or two-way radios to communicate with teachers.

Australia's most famous animal is found in the outback. Do you know what it is? Write its name on the line. Its baby is called a joey.

_____

Many unusual animals live in Australia. Start in the center of the maze and trace a path to each one.

Koala
This animal has sharp claws that help it climb trees.

Kookaburra
This bird's call sounds like a loud laugh.

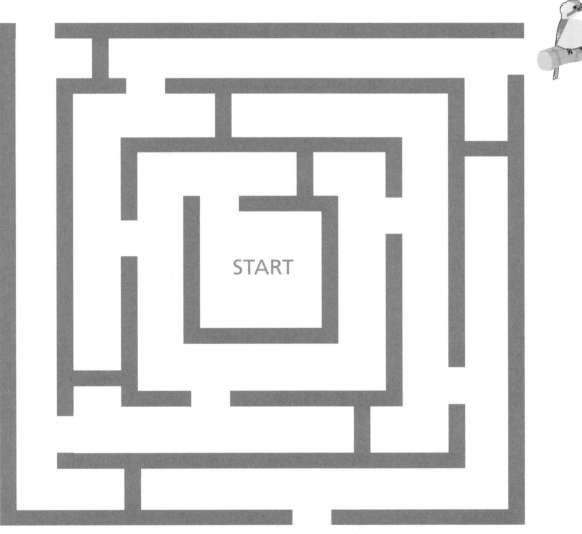

START

Platypus
The snout of this animal looks like a duck's bill.

The native people of Australia are called Aborigines (say AB-ur-IJ-uh-nees). Thousands of years ago, they created paintings of animals on cave walls. Often they painted the outline of an animal, then filled it with many dots.

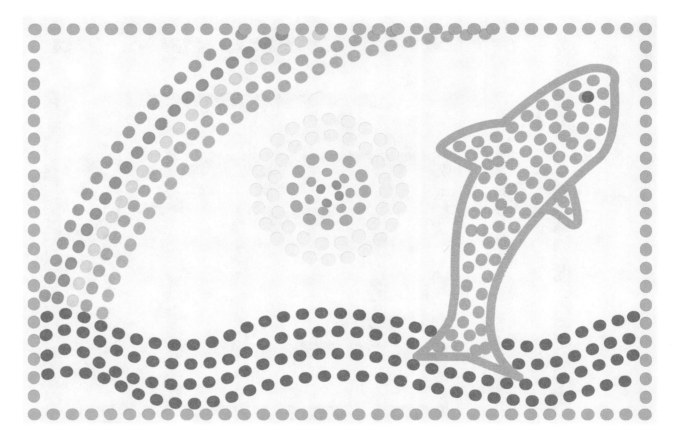

You can make a drawing that looks like the Aborigines' paintings. You will need a piece of paper and some markers or crayons.

1. Draw the outline of an animal on the paper.

2. Using the tip of a marker or crayon, fill in the animal with many small dots.

People from England came to live in Australia about two hundred years ago. Many ways of life in Australia today are based on English customs. However, Australians have many words that are different from those in other English-speaking countries.

Australian Word Meaning

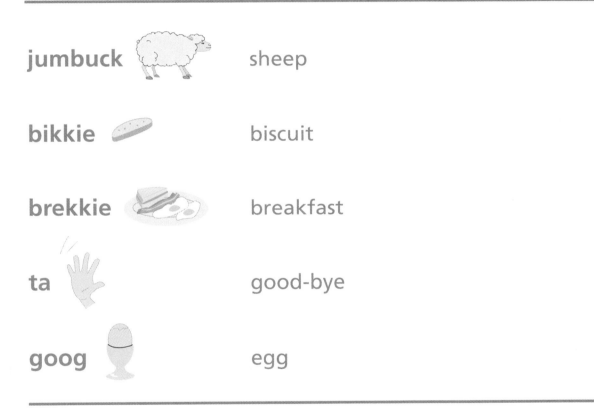

jumbuck   sheep

bikkie   biscuit

brekkie   breakfast

ta   good-bye

goog   egg

What does this sentence mean? Write down what it means on the lines below.

I like to have googs and bikkies for brekkie.

_____

_____

Australia is divided into eight states and territories. The A.C.T. is the Australian Capital Territory. It is the home of Australia's capital city, Canberra.

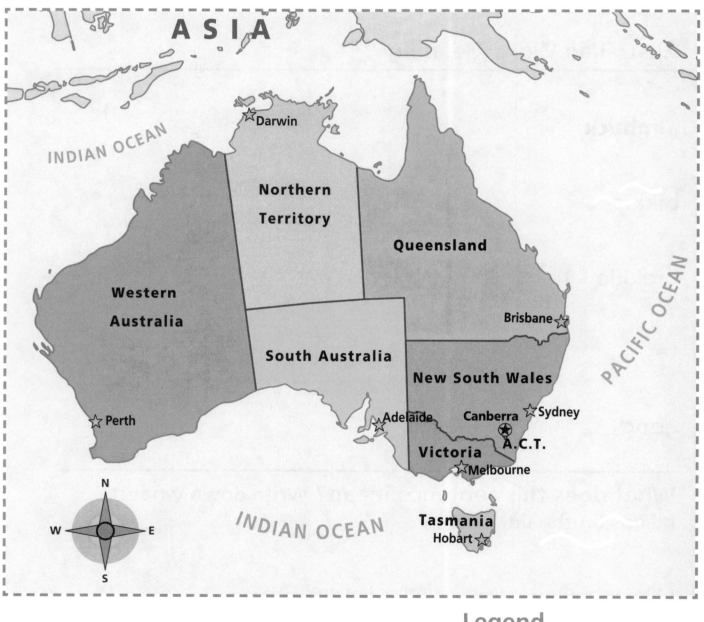

Legend

⊛ National Capital

☆ State Capital

— State Boundary

Match each of these cities with its state or territory.

___ **1**. Perth   **a**. South Australia

___ **2**. Brisbane   **b**. Victoria

___ **3**. Sydney   **c**. Western Australia

___ **4**. Darwin   **d**. Queensland

___ **5**. Melbourne   **e**. Northern Territory

___ **6**. Hobart   **f**. Australian Capital Territory

___ **7**. Adelaide   **g**. Tasmania

___ **8**. Canberra   **h**. New South Wales

Guess What

Some of Australia's cities started out as colonies for prisoners from England.

Legend

Herding animals

Growing crops

Raising animals

Making products to sell

Hunting

This map shows the different ways people make a living in Australia. You can see that the middle of the continent has an area with no color. That is because few people live in this dry area.

Use the maps on the opposite page to answer the following questions. Write **T** for true or **F** for false.

_____ **1**. People on the island of Tasmania herd animals for living.

_____ **2**. People who raise animals might live in Queensland.

_____ **3**. The places where people make products to sell are all in the middle of the continent.

_____ **4**. The northern part of Australia has areas where people hunt for a living.

Guess What

Australia has many cattle ranches. The cowboys and cowgirls who work there are called "jackaroos" and "jillaroos."

Antarctica is located at the most southern part of Earth. It is very cold and covered by thick ice. Some people visit Antarctica, but no one lives there all the time.

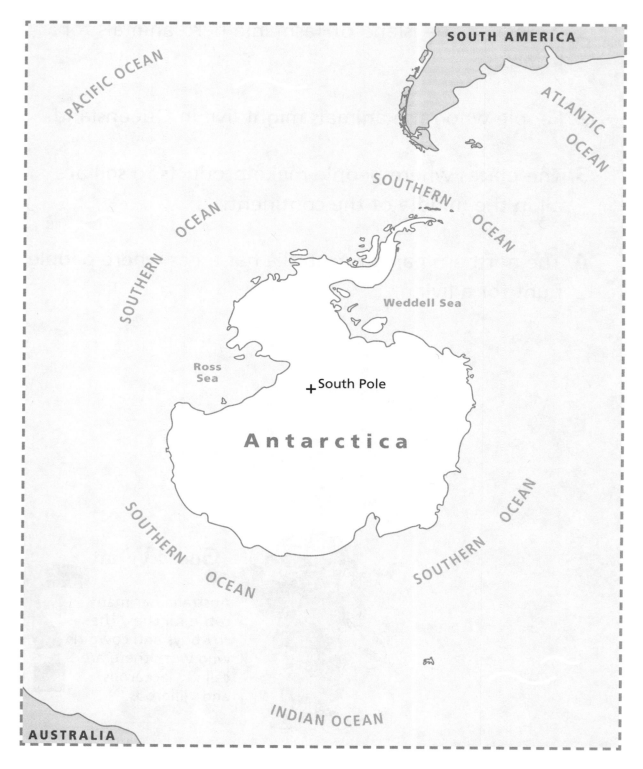

Use the information and the map on the opposite page to help you fill in the blanks below. Some of them have been started for you. When you are done, write the circled letters on the lines at the bottom of the page to answer the riddle.

1. What is the name of the most southern continent on Earth?

___ ___ ___ ___ ___ ___ ___ ___ (◯)

2. What ocean surrounds Antarctica?

___ ___ (◯) ___ ___ ___ ___ (N)

3. What is the name of the pole on Antarctica?

___ ___ ___ (◯) H ___ O ___ ___

4. What are the names of the two seas that border Antarctica?

___ E ___ ___ ___ ___ ___ ___ ___ (◯),

(◯) ___ S ___ ___ ___ ___

5. Antarctica is covered by a thick layer of what? ___ (◯) ___

6. What continent is Antarctica's closest neighbor?

___ O ___ (◯) H ___ M ___ ___ (◯)(◯)(◯)

Who is Uncle Penguin's wife?

___ ___ ___ ___ ___   ___ ___ ___ ___ ___ ___

Many explorers have visited Antarctica. Some parts of Antarctica have been named after these explorers.

Circle these place names on the map below. Then learn about the explorers in the activity on the opposite page.

Ross Sea
Weddell Sea

Learn about explorers of Antarctica. Read the sentences. Then use the code to fill in the missing letters and name the explorers.

CODE

1	2	3	4	5	6	7	8	9	10	11	12	13	14	15	16	17	18	19	20	21	22	23	24	25	26
a	b	c	d	e	f	g	h	i	j	k	l	m	n	o	p	q	r	s	t	u	v	w	x	y	z

1. I was an English explorer who sailed farther south than any earlier explorer.

10	1	13	5	19		23	5	4	4	5	12	12
		m		s			e					l

2. I mapped most of the coast of Antarctica.

10	1	13	5	19		3	12	1	18	11		18	15	19	19
J												R			

Even though it is very cold, Antarctica is home to many kinds of animals.

Krill

Krill are very small animals that live in the ocean.

Whales

An orca is a kind of whale that swims in the waters around Antarctica.

Seals

Seals have a layer of fat to protect them from the cold.

Penguins

Penguins are birds that cannot fly, but they are excellent swimmers.

Fish

Many kinds of fish live in the waters near Antarctica.

Fish in the waters around Antarctica eat krill. Some kinds of penguins eat fish. Some kinds of seals eat penguins. Some kinds of whales eat seals.

Fill in this diagram to show which animals eat which. Draw a picture of each animal or write its name in the box. Use the information above to help you.

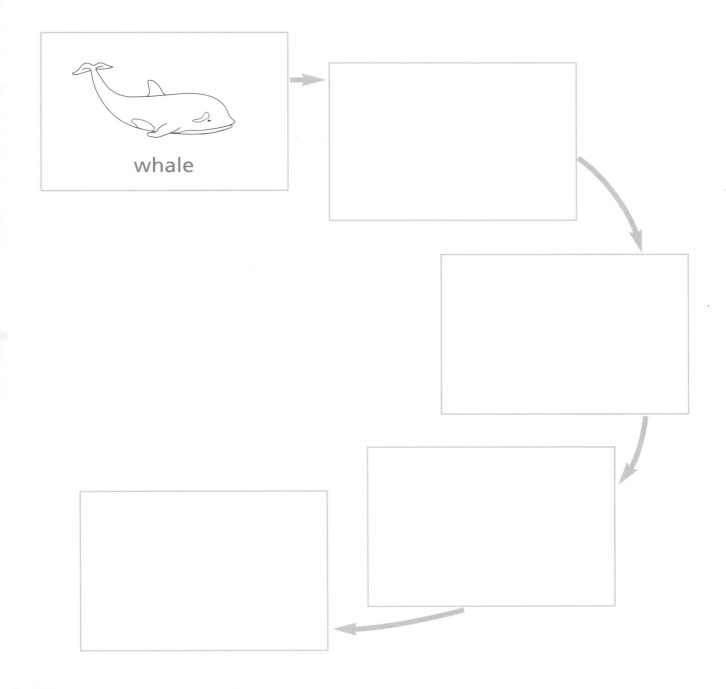

whale

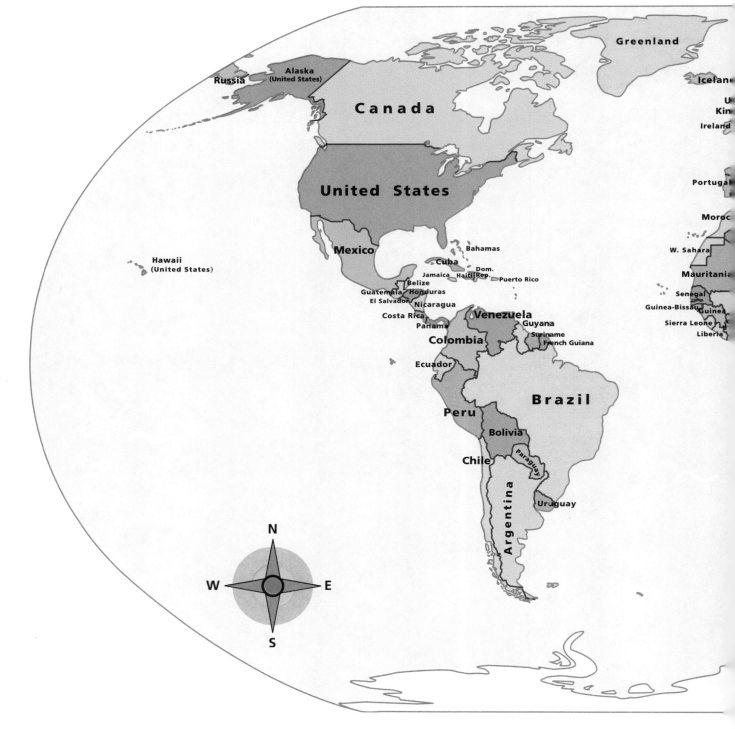

 Many countries do scientific research in Antarctica. Scientists study the continent's climate, animals, and geography.

Here are some countries that have science research stations in Antarctica: **United States, Brazil, China, South Africa.**

On the map, circle the name of each country listed above. Draw a line from each of those countries to Antarctica.

bar scale	the part of a map that tells how much distance on Earth is shown by each inch or millimeter on the map
bird's-eye view	a view of a place from above
climate	how hot, cold, wet, or dry a place is
climate map	a map that shows the kind of weather a place has
compass rose	the part of a map that shows directions
continent	one of the seven largest bodies of land on Earth
country	a land that has a government
desert	a large, dry area of land
directions	North, East, South, West
Eastern Hemisphere	all land and water on the half of Earth that is east of the prime meridian
equator	the line that divides the Northern Hemisphere from the Southern Hemisphere
globe	a model of Earth
hemisphere	half the earth

international boundary	a line on a map that shows where a country begins or ends
island	land that is surrounded by water
landform	a physical feature on the earth's surface with a recognizable shape, such as a mountain or valley
landmass	a large body of land
lines of latitude	lines that run east and west on a map or globe
lines of longitude	lines that run north and south on a map or globe
map	a flat drawing of Earth's surface
map grid	a system of letters and numbers on a map that can be used to locate places
map legend	the part of a map that explains what the symbols mean
map scale	the way distances on a map compare to real distances on Earth
mouth	the place where a river empties into a larger body of water
national capital	the city where a country's government leaders work

Northern Hemisphere	all land and water on the half of Earth that is north of the equator
ocean	one of the five main bodies of water on Earth
peninsula	land that is almost surrounded by water
physical features	places made by nature
physical map	a map that shows natural features and often shows the height of the land
political map	a map that shows how people have divided the land
population map	a map that shows the number of people who live in an area
prime meridian	the line that, along with the 180° line of longitude, divides the Eastern Hemisphere from the Western Hemisphere
rain forest	one of the wettest places on Earth; a rain forest receives at least 100 inches of rain a year
regions	places that have something in common such as climate or traditions
road map	a map that shows highways and streets
route	a way to get from one place to another on a map

sea	a large body of salt water that is smaller than an ocean
source	the place where a river starts
Southern Hemisphere	all land and water on the half of Earth that is south of the equator
state	a part of a country
state boundary	the line on a map that shows where a state begins or ends
state capital	the city where a state's government leaders work
strait	a narrow waterway connecting two larger bodies of water
symbol	a line, color, or shape on a map that stands for something else
thematic map	a map that shows special kinds of information about a place
time zone	one of the parts of Earth that have the same time in common; most time zones have a time that is one hour different from the zones next to it
Western Hemisphere	all land and water on the half of Earth that is west of the prime meridian

Page 5

The meeting place is at the ice cream stand.

Page 6

The picture on the right shows a bird's-eye view.

Page 7

1. classroom
2. highway
3. lake
4. town
5. farm
6. railroad tracks

Page 10

N is for north, s is for south, e is for east, and w is for west.

Page 11

1. Billy's
2. west
3. south

Page 12

The letter e is in section C-2.

A map grid helps you **find a place**.

Page 14

The line should be 5 inches long.

Page 15

About 200 miles

Page 17

1. north
2. Redwing Avenue and Stone Avenue
3. George could walk north on Stone Avenue and west on Hill Street. He could also walk north on Stone Avenue, west on Water Street, and north on First Avenue. There are other routes, too. Did you find a different one?
4. The pet shop

Page 19

1. political map
2. physical map

Page 23

1. M
2. G
3. B
4. G
5. B

Page 25

1. e
2. b
3. d
4. f
5. c
6. a

Page 27

1. Pacific Ocean
2. Atlantic Ocean
3. Arctic Ocean
4. Indian Ocean
5. Southern Ocean

Page 29

Canada
Mexico

Page 31

The equator crosses South America, Africa, and Asia.
The prime meridian crosses Europe, Africa, and Antarctica.

Page 35

The line at 0° longitude is the prime meridian.

Page 36

South America

Page 37

1. Pacific Ocean
2. Asia
3. Australia
4. South America
5. North America

A latitude and longitude location is an **earth** address.

Page 39

Five o'clock

Page 43
1. British Columbia
2. Prince Edward Island
3. Hudson Bay
4. Ontario
5. Ottawa

Page 45
1. c
2. d
3. e
4. a
5. f
6. b

Page 47
1. Washington, D.C.
2. Springfield

Page 49
1. Kansas
2. Minnesota
3. Florida

Page 51
1. California
2. Texas
3. Florida
4. Nevada
5. Louisiana
6. Montana

Page 52
HOMES

Page 55
Boston: mittens and snow boots
Phoenix: jacket
Miami: shorts and an umbrella

Page 57
1. Southwest
2. Northeast
3. Midwest
4. South
5. Rocky Mountain
6. Great Plains
7. Pacific
8. Mid-Atlantic

Page 59
Thousands of tulips are in bloom during the Tulip Time Festival.
Cheyenne Frontier Days includes nine rodeos.
Visitors at the St. Paul Winter Carnival can see a palace carved out of ice.

Page 60
1. Mexico City
2. Belize and Guatemala
3. south

Page 65
1. Brazil
2. Bolivia and Paraguay
3. Ecuador and Brazil

Page 67
escuela (school) – escola
zapatos (shoes) – sapatas
libro (book) – livro

Page 69
1. Buenos Aires
2. Bogota
3. Brasilia
4. Lima
5. Caracas

Page 71
```
H I E Z L K
E R J F L G
N L A D A S
T O G J M H
T O U C A N
B M A Q B V
J E R D J C
```

Page 75
1. Finland
2. Spain
3. Italy

Page 78
Less crowded

Page 81

Across
1. Ural
3. Apennines
6. Thames

Down
2. Alps
4. Pyrenees
5. Volga

Page 85
1. north
2. a boat ticket
3. Europe

Page 87
camel – desert
colobus monkey – forest
hippo – river

Page 91
The route through the Suez Canal is shorter.

Page 93
1. d
2. a
3. b
4. e
5. c

Page 95
1. Arctic Ocean, Pacific Ocean,
   Indian Ocean
2. Russia

Page 96
1. fireworks
2. kite
3. paper

Page 99
1. Russia
2. Mongolia
3. Japan

Page 101
Four: Russia, Kazakhstan, Azerbaijan, and Turkey.

Page 103
elephant

Page 105
1. east
2. Canberra
3. Indian Ocean

Page 106
Kangaroo

Page 109
I like to have eggs and biscuits for breakfast.

Page 111
1. c
2. d
3. h
4. e
5. b
6. g
7. a
8. f

Page 113
1. False
2. True
3. False
4. True

Page 115
1. Antarctica
2. Southern
3. South Pole
4. Weddell Sea, Ross Sea
5. Ice
6. South America

Uncle Penguin's wife is **Aunt Arctica**.

Page 117
1. James Weddell
2. James Clark Ross

Page 119
whales → seals → penguins → fish → krill